P9-DHP-999

You're Already Amazing
LifeGrowth Guide

Other Books by Holley Gerth

You're Already Amazing

You're Made for a God-Sized Dream

Opening the Door to Your God-Sized Dreams

You're Going to Be Okay

What Your Heart Needs for the Hard Days

You're Loved No Matter What

You're Already Amazing

LifeGrowth Guide

Embracing Who You Are,
Becoming All God Created You to Be

Holley Gerth

Revell

a division of Baker Publishing Group
Grand Rapids, Michigan

© 2016 by Holley, Inc.

Published by Revell
a division of Baker Publishing Group
P.O. Box 6287, Grand Rapids, MI 49516-6287
www.revellbooks.com

Printed in the United States of America

All rights reserved. No part of this publication may be reproduced, stored in a retrieval system, or transmitted in any form or by any means—for example, electronic, photocopy, recording—without the prior written permission of the publisher. The only exception is brief quotations in printed reviews.

Library of Congress Cataloging-in-Publication Data
Names: Gerth, Holley.
Title: You're already amazing LifeGrowth guide : embracing who you are, becoming all God created you to be / Holley Gerth.
Description: Grand Rapids, MI : Revell Books, 2016. | Includes bibliographical references.
Identifiers: LCCN 2015040484 | ISBN 9780800726966 (pbk.)
Subjects: LCSH: Christian women—Religious life—Textbooks. | Self-acceptance in women—
Classification: LCC BV4527 .G46625 2016 | DDC 155.2—dc23 LC record available at http://lccn.loc.gov/2015040484

Some material in this book is taken from *You're Already Amazing* (Revell, 2012).

Unless otherwise indicated, Scripture quotations are from the Holy Bible, New International Version®. NIV®. Copyright © 1973, 1978, 1984, 2011 by Biblica, Inc.™ Used by permission of Zondervan. All rights reserved worldwide. www.zondervan.com

Scripture quotations labeled KJV are from the King James Version of the Bible.

Scripture quotations labeled NIV 1984 are from the Holy Bible, New International Version®. NIV®. Copyright © 1973, 1978, 1984 by Biblica, Inc.™ Used by permission of Zondervan. All rights reserved worldwide. www.zondervan.com

Scripture quotations labeled NKJV are from the New King James Version. Copyright © 1982 by Thomas Nelson, Inc. Used by permission. All rights reserved.

Scripture quotations labeled NLT are from the *Holy Bible*, New Living Translation, copyright © 1996, 2004, 2007 by Tyndale House Foundation. Used by permission of Tyndale House Publishers, Inc., Carol Stream, Illinois 60188. All rights reserved.

Italics in Scripture quotations are the author's emphasis.

16 17 18 19 20 21 22   7 6 5 4 3 2 1

In keeping with biblical principles of creation stewardship, Baker Publishing Group advocates the responsible use of our natural resources. As a member of the Green Press Initiative, our company uses recycled paper when possible. The text paper of this book is composed in part of post-consumer waste.

Contents

The Dare

Pssst . . . pull up a chair and I'll tell you a secret. You'd better lean in close for this one.

Ready?

You don't have to *do* more, *be* more, *have* more.

I'm sure there are security alarms going off somewhere. You should probably hide this book when your in-laws come over. And this could be the makings of a Sunday morning scandal.

But it's true.

It's the kind of true that will change your life, set you free, and make you wake up smiling for the first time in a long time. I know because that's what it did for me (and believe me, for this non–morning girl that's nothing short of miraculous). I've seen it happen to a lot of other women too. I've read it in their words through thousands of comments on my blog. I've seen it in their faces on the couch in my counseling office. I've heard it in a new kind of laughter over coffee with friends.

So watch out, sister. If you keep reading, you just might be next.

Even if we've never met, I know this about you: you're a daughter of God, a holy princess, a woman created with strengths you've yet to fully grasp and a story that's still being written by the divine Author himself. And if you really take hold of who you are and what you're called to do, there will be no stopping you. That's because there's no stopping him *in you*—and he's got bigger plans for your life than you've even imagined.

Okay, you've been warned.

If you're feeling brave, I dare you to read on . . .

—Holley Gerth, *You're Already Amazing*

Introduction

Since I first wrote the words you just read from *You're Already Amazing*, almost one hundred thousand women have accepted my dare to embrace who they are and become all God created them to be. As I connected with many of them as an author, life coach, and speaker, I often heard comments like these:

- I want to do *You're Already Amazing* as a study at my church or with a group of friends, but I'm not sure how.
- I'm interested in life coaching so I can apply the message in deeper ways, but I don't have the time or money.
- I'm rereading the book because it helped me so much, and I wish there were even more to go with it.

This LifeGrowth Guide is a response to all of the above. It builds on the foundation of *You're Already Amazing* by giving you everything you need to do the book as a group study. It also offers brand-new concepts and even more ways to apply the message so you feel like you have your own personal life coach every step of the way. And it includes bonus material and activities you won't find anywhere else.

Every session has these elements:

- links to short videos that will guide you through the material
- essential excerpts and overviews of concepts from *You're Already Amazing*
- questions for groups to discuss or individuals to reflect on
- interactive tools based on my training as a counselor and life coach to help you apply what you're reading
- optional creative activities you can do with a group or on your own
- prompts for personal journaling

After connecting with women all over the world, I know this: you're busy, and you need to be sure your time, energy, and financial resources are spent wisely. That's why I'm committed to making sure this LifeGrowth Guide won't just give you more information—it will lead to true transformation.

You really can know who God created you to be and what he's called you to do, and you really can have a realistic plan for pursuing his purpose for you. I know that's true because I've already seen thousands of women's lives changed in powerful ways.

Now it's your turn.

Choosing How to Use the LifeGrowth Guide

There are several different ways you can use the *You're Already Amazing LifeGrowth Guide*. Start by reviewing the following options and choosing the one that fits you best.

1. **Group study**—You can easily use this LifeGrowth Guide for a study with a group. For example, you might do so with your women's ministry at church, a few friends at your favorite coffee shop, neighbors in your living room at home, or co-workers at

your office. At the back of this book are step-by-step outlines for each session that will make facilitating a group simple. Even if you've never facilitated a group before, you can do this! All you need is a willing heart and a desire to encourage others.

2. **Online study**—Internet groups work especially well if the women in your group live in different places or have busy schedules that make it hard to meet in person. You can easily host a group on a site like Facebook. If you'd like help setting up your group as well as recommendations for how to facilitate it, see the "Creating an Online LifeGrowth Group" resource at HolleyGerth.com/amazing.

3. **One-on-one**—Simply asking a close friend, a family member, or someone you're in a mentoring relationship with to go through the LifeGrowth Guide with you can be very effective and enjoyable.

4. **Individually**—*You're Already Amazing* was originally written as a book for individuals, and the LifeGrowth Guide can serve as a helpful companion if you're simply reading the book on your own.

What You'll Need Before You Start

1. A copy of the book *You're Already Amazing: Embracing Who You Are, Becoming All God Created You to Be* (available in stores or online, including at HolleyGerth.com/amazing).

2. Access to a device with an internet connection so you can watch the videos for each session. (If you're in a group, you'll watch the videos when you meet.) You can watch the videos for free or purchase a DVD of the videos at HolleyGerth.com/amazing.

3. A pen for answering questions, taking notes, and journaling. If you are using the ebook version, you will need a journal or

notebook for writing answers to the questions and completing the exercises.

4. If you'd like to do the optional creative activity at the end of each session, you'll need a few additional supplies along the way. All of them are easy to find and inexpensive (for example, colored paper, markers).

A Prayer Before We Begin

I wish I could be there to pray for and with you in person, so I'm sending these words in my place:

God,

I thank you for the woman who's reading these words right now. Out of all the places and times in history, you have her here and now for a reason.

I believe you've led her to this LifeGrowth Guide for a purpose. You've heard the questions she's whispered in the quiet of her own heart. You've seen the struggles she's faced. You've listened as she asked you for help. You love her and you want the very best for her.

We live in a world that would like to distract us from our true identities and the purpose you have for us. Please let your voice be the one she hears the loudest and clearest as she goes through the pages that follow.

In everything we do in our time together—as we look at our strengths and skills, as we discover your purpose for us, as we take brave new steps—may all of it ultimately lead to us loving you, others, and ourselves more than ever before. That's what matters most.

We know that you are the only one who can create true growth and change. So we agree right now that this is not about us "trying harder" or "doing more." Instead, it's about a relationship with you. We place ourselves in your hands and invite you to do the work only you can in us.

We humbly affirm that all we are and all we have is a gift from you. Everything amazing about us is because of you, our beyond-amazing God.

In Jesus's name,

Amen.

P.S.: If you'd like to find out more about having a relationship with God, see the Connecting with God section in the back of this book.

Sharing the Journey

I'd love to connect with you! You can find me in these places and let me know you're doing the *You're Already Amazing LifeGrowth Guide*:

Blog: www.holleygerth.com

Facebook: Holley Gerth (author page)

Twitter: @HolleyGerth

Instagram: holleygerth

Pinterest: Holley Gerth

Hashtag: #alreadyamazing

Session 1

Who God Created Us to Be

Groups

Facilitators: See the outlines in the back of the book for recommendations on how to go through this session with your group.

Members: Read chapters 1 and 2 of *You're Already Amazing* and work through this session (except for watching the videos) on your own before you meet.

Introduction

"I'm so exhausted."

"I feel like I've lost who I really am."

"It seems like I'm just going through the motions."

▶ **START THE SESSION 1 VIDEO** on your DVD or online at HolleyGerth.com /amazing.

I hear quiet confessions like these everywhere I go. At coffee with friends. After speaking engagements. When I read my email. Here's what I know is true: *women are tired of trying harder.*

We've done our best to love Jesus as well as our family and friends. We've worked hard to be good. We've worn ourselves out doing what everyone else wants. The problem isn't our lack of effort—it's that no matter what we do, nothing seems to change.

But it doesn't have to be that way. We don't have to live exhausted, stressed-out lives. When Jesus promised life to the full, he meant it (see John 10:10). Researcher Marcus Buckingham did a study with thousands of women to find out what made them thrive. To his surprise, he discovered the number one influence on a woman's well-being is how much time she spends in her "sweet spot." In other words, how closely she stays connected to who God truly made her to be.

In my work as a counselor, life coach, author, and speaker, I've found the same to be true. It's not that women set out to destroy themselves. They simply drift. And like a swimmer in the ocean, they look up one day to find they're miles from where they're meant to be.

Being disconnected from who you really are leads to depression, anxiety, relationship difficulties, and a host of other troubles. Sometimes it can even be fatal. And contrary to popular belief, women who understand and are secure in their true identities are *less selfish*, not more. Being free from insecurity allows us to serve and offer the world what only we can.

Discovering who God made us to be is a lifelong process, and every step of the way we'll be tempted to be like someone else. Why? *Because the enemy of our souls wants us to be like anyone but Jesus.* We are closest to and most like Jesus when we are fully being who he created us to be.

What I'm asking you to do is hard. It's much easier to learn a new fact than to look inside your heart. What I'm asking you to do is scary. It's much less frightening to let someone else tell you who you are than to embrace who God made you to be. What I'm asking you to do is inconvenient. It's much simpler to wake up every day and let life pull you wherever it wants than to cling to God's will.

But what I'm asking you to do is also essential. You will not thrive, fulfill your God-given purpose, or offer what only you can if you don't know who you are. And I'm confident you can do this. You're a warrior and overcomer. You have more strength than it may seem like right now. And you serve a God bigger than you can see.

It's time to stop being so tired.

It's time to discover our true identities.

It's time for us to really believe we're already amazing.

Your *Life Coach*

Sarah says over the phone, "I'm really excited about going through *You're Already Amazing* with you! What's the right way to do this?" I smile and respond, "There's no 'perfect' way to answer the questions or go through this material. Release all the pressure you're feeling to Jesus and just embrace the process." I can hear her take a deep breath, and then she laughs and says, "Okay, this is going to be new territory for me!"

If you're used to doing studies where every question has a correct response, this LifeGrowth Guide may stretch you in ways you haven't experienced before. Whenever we try to grow or change, it's normal to encounter internal resistance. You may feel unsure or insecure at certain points, and that's totally okay. Be gentle with yourself, ask for encouragement when you need it, and keep pressing forward a little at a time. It will be worth it!

Question 1: If you had coffee with a friend today and she asked how you were *really* doing, what would you say?

really doing fine ~ a little restless about what I should be doing & where God wants me to serve, etc.

You created my inmost being;
>*you knit me together in my*
>> *mother's womb.*
I praise you because I am fearfully and wonderfully made;
> *your works are wonderful,*
>> *I know that full well.*

Psalm 139:13–14

What I've discovered through connecting with thousands of women is that we're great at encouraging everyone else, but we're hesitant to do the same for ourselves. But God loves us all the same, and it hurts him just as much when you talk negatively to yourself as it would if you were saying those unkind words about someone else. Here's a challenge for you as you work through this LifeGrowth Guide: *don't say anything to or about yourself that you wouldn't say to someone you love.*

Who am I?

It's a question we ask throughout our lives. Oh, maybe we don't use those exact words. But we're looking for the answer from the time we awkwardly enter the middle school cafeteria and hope for a table where we belong. It can drive us to fix our hair a certain way, date that boy, break that rule, join that club, or pursue that degree, and it can ultimately take us to the life we have now. Even as grown women, we still ask it. We just trade the junior high cafeteria for a women's retreat,

With *Jesus*

We're not only *amazing*.

We're *enough*.

We're *beautiful*.

We're *wanted*.

We're *chosen*.

We're *called*.

We've got what it takes . . .

not just to survive but to

change the world.

—Holley Gerth

Print or pass along this word art through the "Share the Love" section of HolleyGerth.com/amazing.

corporate boardroom, or playgroup. No matter how many years go by, we still ask, "Who am I, *really*?"

And until we can answer that question, it's impossible to believe we're amazing.

I believe the desire to know who we really are has been placed within us by the heart of heaven itself. God wants us to understand who he created us to be so that we can fulfill the purpose he has for our lives. Sometimes we feel guilty for wishing we knew more about ourselves. After all, we're not supposed to focus on ourselves, right? I often hear women say, "That's selfish." But it's not the question that matters—it's what we do with the answer.

If you want to understand yourself just so that you can do whatever you'd like for your personal gain, then it's self-centered. If your intent is to love God, others, and yourself more, then knowing who you are is one of the most unselfish things you can do. And I have a feeling that second option is why you're reading this book. Yes? So push that guilt aside and give yourself permission to explore who God made you to be.

—*You're Already Amazing*, chapter 2

Question 2: What do you think makes it so hard for women to believe they're already amazing?

easy to feel we should/could do more, how are we growing & bettering ourselves? Does anyone ever feel they have it all together + perfectly figured out? But, we can know that God loves us + that is the most important thing!

Your *Life Coach*

I'm standing at the front of a room with tables full of women, explaining that we're about to go through exercises that will help us figure out our strengths, our skills, and who God made us to be. I notice a worried look in the back corner followed by a hand quietly raised and a question asked: "I want to do this, but I'm afraid it's not humble. What if I'm being prideful?"

I'm often called on for reassurance that pride doesn't have any place in this process. And I can certainly understand that concern, because I struggled with a fear of accidentally "becoming prideful" for many years. It bothered me so much I finally decided to look at Scripture to see what true humility means. Most of the time, the word *humility* is from the Hebrew word *kana*, which implies submission to another's will. In the New Testament, it's a Greek word formed from two others: *tapeinos* (low to the ground) and *phren* (our hearts/minds). Put all of that together, and humility means bowing our hearts to God. Or in other words, submitting to his will. And that means agreeing with what he says and living it out—*including what he says about us*. Our strengths and skills are more than personal characteristics; they're messages that tell us who God made us.

It's never God's intention for us to go through life with our heads hanging down in insecurity and hearts made heavy by fear we're not enough. "Humble yourselves before the Lord, and *he will lift you up*" (James 4:10). We come to God and say, "I bow my heart before you in love. You are God and I am not. All I am, all I have is yours." Then he responds, "Stand tall, my daughter. You are loved. You are of great worth. Do my will." That's what living in true humility looks like, and it's the ultimate goal for the exercises we're about to go through together.

Find Your Strengths

Strength: a personal characteristic that can be used on behalf of God in service to others.

Circle or highlight at least three strengths that apply to you.

- Adventurous
- Athletic
- Brave
- Calm
- Capable
- Caring
- Cheerful
- Considerate
- Courageous
- Creative
- Dedicated
- Determined
- Devoted
- Easygoing
- Efficient
- Encouraging
- Energetic
- Fair

- Flexible
- Forgiving
- Friendly
- Frugal
- Funny
- Gentle
- Gracious
- Hardworking
- Helpful
- Honest
- Hospitable
- Imaginative
- Intelligent
- Kind
- Loving
- Loyal
- Mature
- Organized

- Positive
- Protective
- Reflective
- Reliable
- Resilient
- Resourceful
- Responsible
- Sensitive
- Servant-hearted
- Spontaneous
- Supportive
- Talented
- Thoughtful
- Trustworthy
- Warm
- Wise
- *Add your own . . .*

Tip: If you're not sure what your strengths are, ask at least one other person for input. You can do this face-to-face or through a written message like, "I'm doing a LifeGrowth Guide to find out more about who God made me to be, and I'd love to have your feedback. What are three strengths you see in me?" Watch for patterns in people's responses, and if the words they use aren't on the list provided, feel free to add them.

If you're not sure something is really a strength for you, you can also put it through the STRENGTH test. Choose a word you circled on the strengths list, then answer yes or no for each question below.

Service—Does it help me serve God and others?

Time—Has it been present throughout much of my life?

Relationships—Do others see this?

Energy—Do I feel energized when I'm living this way?

Natural—Does this come naturally to me most of the time? *Or do I know God has intentionally developed this in me even though it doesn't?*

Glory—Does God ultimately get the glory from it?

Trials—Even in hard times, does it usually come through somehow?

Heart—Does this really feel like a core part of who I am?

If you answered "yes" to most of the questions, then the word you circled is one of your strengths.

Question 3: What are your top three strengths and an example of how God uses each one? (Example: Friendly—I'm usually one of the first people to say hi to someone new.)

Question 4: We often think of weaknesses as a negative thing. But the research shared in *You're Already Amazing* shows that having weaknesses in certain areas actually helps us to be stronger in others. God also says that his "strength is made perfect in weakness" (2 Cor. 12:9 NKJV). What's a weakness you wish you didn't have? In what ways could it actually help you be who God created you to be? (Example: Being weak at details helps make me strong at seeing the big picture.)

_____

_____

_____

For we are God's handiwork, created in Christ Jesus to do good works, which God prepared in advance for us to do. (Eph. 2:10)

Find Your Skills

Now that you know your strengths, what should you do with them? Chances are, you're already doing something. Strengths are made to be expressed. We call those expressions *skills*. Our skills are given to us by God, and they matter to him. In fact, the first time the Spirit is mentioned in relation to a person in Scripture, it is in a verse that talks about skills. In describing a craftsman chosen to work on the tabernacle, God says, "I have filled him with the Spirit of God, with skill, ability and knowledge in all kinds of crafts" (Exod. 31:3 NIV 1984).

Skill: a strength expressed in a specific way that builds up others and benefits the kingdom.

Circle or highlight at least three skills that apply to you.

○ Acting	○ Decorating	○ Persevering
○ Adapting	○ Empathizing	○ Persuading
○ Administering	○ Encouraging	○ Planning
○ Advising	○ Evaluating	○ Prioritizing
○ Analyzing	○ Expressing	○ Problem-solving
○ Appreciating	○ Growing	○ Protecting
○ Assembling	○ Guiding	○ Relating
○ Believing	○ Helping	○ Responding
○ Building	○ Imagining	○ Risk taking
○ Challenging	○ Influencing	○ Serving
○ Cleaning	○ Initiating	○ Sharing
○ Collaborating	○ Leading	○ Speaking
○ Cooking	○ Listening	○ Supporting
○ Communicating	○ Maintaining	○ Teaching
○ Connecting	○ Managing	○ Training
○ Constructing	○ Motivating	○ Writing
○ Coordinating	○ Negotiating	○ *Add your own . . .*
○ Counseling	○ Nurturing	
○ Creating	○ Organizing	

Tip: She sets another dish on the counter, then turns to me and says, "I don't think I have any skills. At least not like you do." I point to a beautiful table already piled high with tantalizing food and ask, "What's all this?" She waves a hand through the air dismissively and responds, "This is nothing. It was simple." I smile then shake my head and say, "It would have taken me weeks to do what you threw together in a couple of hours. Cooking, decorating, and hospitality are three fabulous skills, and you're welcome to practice them with me anytime you'd like!"

My friend's two phrases "This is nothing" and "It was simple" are twin clues that skills are hiding somewhere in plain sight. When something seems natural for us, we assume it's the same for others. But most likely it's an indication of a unique God-given ability. What are you doing when people compliment you and you can't quite understand why they think it's a big deal? Be sure those are included on your skills chart. If nothing comes to mind right away, that's okay. Just begin watching for those moments and come back to this exercise. Like we talked about with your strengths, you can also ask others for their input.

Question 5: What are your top three skills, and what's an example of how God uses each of them? (Example: Decorating—I create spaces where people feel welcome and loved.)

Connecting Your Strengths and Skills

Skills circles can be a fun way to connect strengths with skills. You put one of your strengths in the middle of a big circle. Then smaller circles around the edge represent the skills related to that strength. Here's a personal example:

The size of each circle is related to how much I express that strength through the skill. For example, I write a lot more than I speak.

Now you give it a try. Have fun with this! You can use the figure provided, draw on a blank piece of paper, or put skills circles in your journal. This isn't meant to be a big project—just a little tool.

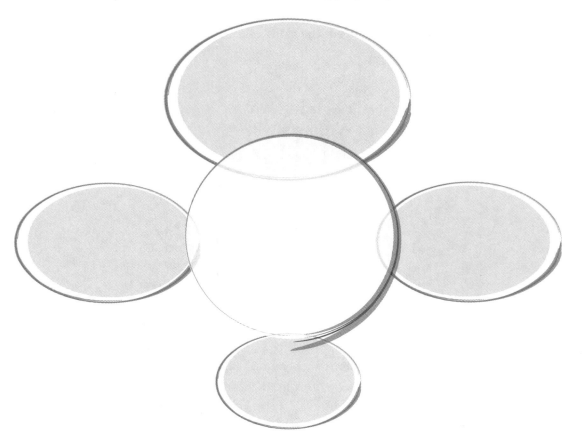

Whatever you do, do it all for the glory of God.
(1 Cor. 10:31)

Once you know your strengths (who you are) and skills (what you do) as well as understand the relationships in your life, you're ready to explore who you're specifically called to serve. You can start by taking a look at who's already in your life.

Your Social Circles

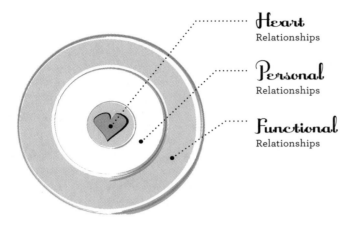

Heart
Relationships

Personal
Relationships

Functional
Relationships

Heart Relationships—This is your inner circle, those with whom you can truly share who you are, the ups and downs. Some family members and your close friends would be here.

Personal Relationships—These people share your life in your neighborhood, church, work, family, and so on. You care about each other, but they are more casual relationships than the first group.

Functional Relationships—These connections are very casual, and interactions have a practical purpose. You might call them acquaintances.

Think about names that would be in each of your circles and write them in the following figure or in your journal if you'd like. For example, if Paige is your best friend, put her name in the Heart Relationships circle. You don't have to include everyone you know—just enough to give you a broad overview of who's in your life and how you're connecting to others.

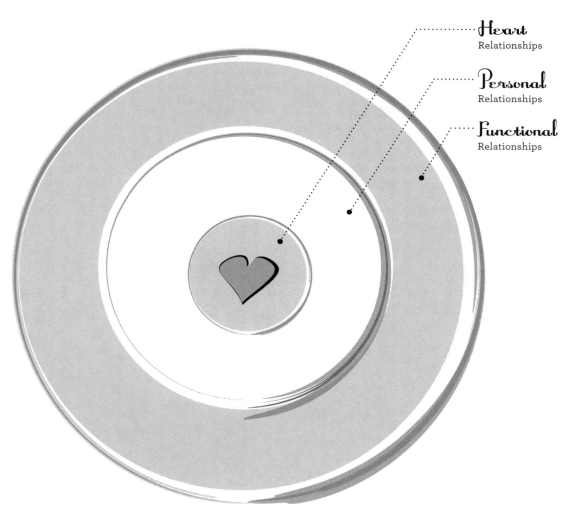

Heart
Relationships

Personal
Relationships

Functional
Relationships

Your *Life Coach*

In *You're Already Amazing* I shared a study reporting that 50 percent of Americans do not have even one friend they can confide in. So if you wrote even one name in the previous exercise, then you're doing well.

It's normal for our relationships to fluctuate in different seasons of life. Moves, job changes, and life transitions like having a baby can throw our social circles for a loop. When that happens we tend to tell ourselves, "I'm the only one going through this" or even "Something must be wrong with me." Try to resist both of those thoughts and instead realize that relationships in a broken, fallen world with broken, fallen people are tricky for everyone. We all experience loneliness at times.

You may find it really freeing to pray, "God, I entrust all of my relationships to you. You've created me to share life with others, so please connect me with the people you want in my life for this season."

Find Your Who

Sometimes a group of people also has a special place in our hearts. You might love working with kids, women, older adults, or inner-city youth. Knowing your *who* can help you make strategic choices about which opportunities to pursue and which to pass up. These questions will help you learn more about who you may be called to serve.

I feel especially drawn to:

_____

_____

I'm at my best when I'm with:

_____

_____

God has given me a tender spot in my heart for:

_____

_____

My strengths and skills seem to help:

_____

_____

Tip: What you wrote might be very general (for example, "my family" or "women"), or it might be very specific ("children with special needs under the age of five"). Either way is okay.

Also, your *who* may change throughout your life. Right now you might be focused on toddlers because you've got three of them! Later on, you might shift your focus to mentoring college students.

It's also okay if you don't find a specific *who* right now. As mentioned before, we're all called to love each other. So if nothing comes to mind here, just serve whoever is in your life right now!

Question 6: Who has God placed in your life during this season for you to serve? How are you already doing so?

_____

_____

_____

"Love the Lord your God with all your heart and with all your soul and with all your mind." This is the first and greatest commandment. And the second is like it: "Love your neighbor as yourself." (Matt. 22:37–39)

When an opportunity that seems to fit with your strengths, your skills, and your who comes along, you can use the tools in this section as filters to see if it's really in the center of what you're created to do. If it is, you can be fairly sure God is giving you the green light! If not, ask him if he specifically wants you to accept it as a special assignment that's outside of what you're called to do most of the time.

Later in the LifeGrowth Guide, we'll combine the pieces you worked on in this session to create a LIFE statement. So if you haven't completed all the exercises in this session, continue thinking and praying about them and do so soon.

your strengths + your skills + who you're called to serve = making a difference in the world in your own amazing way

—Holley Gerth

Your *Life Coach*

Sheila happily circles strengths and skills, then writes down who she feels called to serve. With renewed energy, she returns from her lunch break and drops her purse on her desk. As she does so, a haphazard stack of paper topples and lands on a folder she's been meaning to go through for weeks. Suddenly Sheila's thoughts feel scattered too.

"How could I ever have circled 'organizing' on that skills list?" she mutters under her breath.

The reality is, none of us live in a perfect world. And none of us are perfect people. Even when it comes to our strengths and skills, we will have times when we falter. Or seasons when life makes it all but impossible to live them out. When that happens, extend grace to yourself. For example, Sheila needs to remember that her company's recent merger has everyone in chaos. And her unrelenting focus on keeping her team organized means her desk isn't getting as much of that skill as it usually does.

Strengths, skills, and who we're called to serve show up as patterns over many years. Don't judge them by a challenging moment or hard day. When you find yourself getting away from who you're created to be, simply ask God to gently bring you back. He's the One who will encourage, equip, and empower you for a lifetime.

Your Next Step: What's one truth or aha moment you got from this session? What's one way you'll use it in your life this week?

RESUME THE SESSION 1 VIDEO on your DVD or online at HolleyGerth.com /amazing.

MORE LIFEGROWTH

Pick your favorite, do them all, or add your own.

Connect

Share what's on your heart after completing this session.

Blog: www.holleygerth.com
Facebook: Holley Gerth (author page)
Twitter: @HolleyGerth
Instagram: holleygerth
Pinterest: Holley Gerth
Hashtag: #alreadyamazing

Get Creative

Make a collage that represents your strengths, your skills, and who you're called to serve. You can use magazines, photos, images printed from online, or whatever materials you already have. Try to make it messy and imperfect. Save a spot on it for your LIFE statement, which you'll complete in Session 5.

You can do the collage on one of the blank Get Creative pages in the back of the LifeGrowth Guide or on separate paper.

If you're in a group that's doing these activities, your facilitator will let you know if you should do this before you meet or if you'll complete this project together.

I'd love for you to take a photo of your collage and share it with me on Facebook or Instagram. You can also use the hashtag #alreadyamazing.

Journal

One of the most powerful passages of Scripture about who God created us to be and how intimately he knows us is found in Psalm 139. Read that Psalm and write a prayer praising God and thanking him for who he has made you.

You can use the Notes and Journaling pages in the back of the LifeGrowth Guide or your personal journal.

Go Deeper

If you'd like more questions for group discussion or personal reflection, see the Go Deeper Guide included in *You're Already Amazing*. You can download a printable version at HolleyGerth.com/amazing.

Session 2

What's True No Matter How We Feel

Groups

Facilitators: See the outlines in the back of the book for recommendations on how to go through this session with your group.

Members: Read chapters 3 and 4 of *You're Already Amazing* and go through this session (except for watching the videos) on your own before you meet.

Introduction

The next two topics we're covering—truth and emotions—both have one source: *our hearts*. As I'm writing this, Valentine's Day is quickly

START THE SESSION 2 VIDEO on your DVD or online at HolleyGerth.com /amazing.

approaching. It seems everywhere I turn I see displays full of heart-shaped balloons, bouquets of flowers, boxes of candy, and other declarations of love. Our culture primarily associates the heart with romance. But in the ancient world, the heart had a far more complex role.

The heart is mentioned over one thousand times in Scripture, and it "denotes a person's center for both physical and emotional-intellectual-moral activities."[1] In other words, our heart is the core of who we are. As Proverbs 4:23 says, "Everything you do flows from it."

Our hearts are where we hold truth:

The word is very near you; it is in your mouth and in your *heart* so you may obey it. (Deut. 30:14)

I have hidden your word in my *heart* that I might not sin against you. (Ps. 119:11)

I will put my laws in their *hearts*. (Heb. 10:16)

Our hearts are also susceptible to lies, and they have been from the very beginning. When we believe those lies, we lose our freedom and joy. God wants to give both back to us, and that's what we're going to invite him to do during our time together.

The scene is set. God has created the world in seven glorious days. Adam and Eve live in Paradise. And then the devil shows up with a single question: "Did God really say . . . ?" (Gen. 3:1). Insecurity makes its debut. Eve responds, then reconsiders. "The woman was convinced" (Gen. 3:6 NLT).

Everything changes forever.

I find it interesting that the enemy didn't blatantly tempt Eve. He didn't ask, "So, how about we head off to Las Vegas and run wild?" He was much more subtle. And his question is hauntingly familiar. I've heard other versions:

"Did God really say you have what it takes?"

"Did God really say you're loved?"

"Did God really say who you are is okay?"

And, like Eve, I often respond, reconsider, and become convinced. What if Eve had said, "Yep, God sure did say that, and I'm not listening to another word. Hit the road, buster"?

What if *we* said that?

"Yes, God really did say I can do all things through Christ" (see Phil. 4:13).

"Yes, God really did say he loves me with an everlasting love" (see Jer. 31:3).

"Yes, God really did say I am fearfully and wonderfully made" (see Ps. 139:14).

Everything could change forever.

—*You're Already Amazing*, chapter 3

Your *Life Coach*

I stare at the computer screen and tentatively begin typing. I'm in an online group of women I know is a safe space. As I describe a struggle I'm facing, the soundtrack in my mind keeps repeating, "What's wrong with you? You just need to get over this."

But the responses that quickly come in the form of comments sound completely different. In just a few minutes, I feel so much better. My friends extend grace and truth to me when I can't find the strength to offer them to myself.

There will be moments when the lies in your heart are so loud that you can't even seem to declare the truth. That happens to all of us. And when it does, it's okay to ask someone else to remind you of what's true.

When Eve was tempted in the Garden of Eden, Scripture reveals, Adam was right there beside her. What if she had paused and said to him, "I'm feeling confused right now. What did God say is really true?" We'll never know the answer to that question, but it could have altered the entire story of humanity.

Doubt and lies thrive in the dark. Bring them into the light of loving relationships—whether that happens through the bright flicker of a screen, on a phone call, or face-to-face with someone you trust over coffee. When you share what's really going on in your life, you give others permission to do the same. Then, "speaking the truth in love, we will grow to become in every respect the mature body of him who is the head, that is, Christ" (Eph. 4:15).

Identify the Lies

As I've connected with thousands of women around the world as an author, speaker, and life coach, I've discovered many of us are vulnerable to similar lies. Some of the most common ones follow, and we're going to confront them together.

Write a number between 1 and 5 for each of these lies to rate how much you struggle with each one (1 = I never struggle with this lie; 3 = I sometimes struggle with this lie; 5 = this lie is a significant battle in my life).

_____ *Lie #1*: I have to be perfect.

Truth: I've been made "perfect" in God's eyes because of what Jesus did on the cross, and he will help me grow to be more like him until that process is complete in heaven. "He has made perfect forever those who are being made holy" (Heb. 10:14).

_____ *Lie #2*: I need to be more like someone else.

Truth: I only need to be more like Jesus. "Am I now trying to win the approval of human beings, or of God? Or am I trying to please people? If I were still trying to please people, I would not be a servant of Christ" (Gal. 1:10).

_____ *Lie #3*: I don't have anything to offer.

Truth: I have specific gifts, strengths, and skills to contribute to the body of Christ, and I'm irreplaceable. "As each part does its own special work, it helps the other parts grow, so that the whole body is healthy and growing and full of love" (Eph. 4:16 NLT).

_____ *Lie #4*: Being confident will make me prideful and selfish.

Truth: Agreeing with God that I'm "fearfully and wonderfully made" is true humility, which leads to glorifying him and serving others. "I praise you because I am fearfully and wonderfully made; your works are wonderful, I know that full well" (Ps. 139:14).

_____ *Lie #5*: I am who others say I am.

Truth: I am who God says I am, and "there is now no condemnation for those who are in Christ Jesus" (Rom. 8:1).

What's another lie you're tempted to believe? Add it here.

Lie:

_____

_____

Truth (including a Scripture):

_____

_____

Perfectionism is all or nothing.

Growth is little by little.

Perfectionism is all about the goal.

Growth is more about
the journey.

Perfectionism is about outward appearances.

Growth is about
what happens on the inside.

Perfectionism is about what we do.

Growth is about
who we're becoming.

—HOLLEY GERTH

Print or pass along this word art through the "Share the Love" section of HolleyGerth.com/amazing.

Tip: If you want help finding a Scripture to replace the lie you're tempted to believe, you can do a search on a site like BibleGateway .com. Just enter a keyword like *fear*, and it will give you a list of related verses.

Tip: Often the lies we hear within our hearts are so familiar to us that we don't even recognize them. Think about the last time you felt insecure or anxious. What thoughts were going through your mind? Most likely they contained lies in disguise. Negative emotions are excellent lie detectors that usually go off when we believe something untrue. Rather than ignoring your feelings or trying to make them go away immediately, pay attention to the valuable insights they're revealing to you.

Embracing Our Emotions

Our hearts are not only where we hold truth and believe lies; they're also intimately connected to our emotions.

I have great sorrow and unceasing anguish in my *heart*. (Rom. 9:2)

My *heart* is glad. (Ps. 16:9)

Each *heart* knows its own bitterness, and no one else can share its joy. (Prov. 14:10)

One of the most dangerous lies we can believe is that our emotions are inherently wrong or sinful. Emotions are not "bad" or "good." They are simply messengers that God has given us to help us understand what is happening in our lives. We're not to obey them, but we are to be aware of them.

A woman walks into my counseling office. She talks of loss in her life. As tears slip down her cheeks, she grabs a tissue and says, "But I shouldn't feel this way."

Another woman arrives later in the day. She describes abuse and wrongs against her that have left deep scars on her heart. Her voice gets louder until she stops midsentence and says, "But I shouldn't feel this way."

A final client steps through the door and talks of a new opportunity. It's way out of her comfort zone. She starts to explore the unknown, then folds her shaking hands and says, "But I shouldn't feel this way."

I've responded like this too. Emotions knock on the door of my heart, and I turn them away. I hear old lines spoken by well-meaning people, like "If you're not smiling, you won't be a witness for Jesus" or "If you feel fear, you're not showing faith."

But in each of these scenarios, the emotion was just a message about what that woman was experiencing.

For the first woman, sadness was saying, "You've experienced a loss."

For the second, anger was declaring, "You've been wronged."

And for the third, fear was cautioning, "You've got an exciting opportunity—but there are risks involved too."

Those emotions hopefully prompt the first woman to seek comfort, the second to tend to her wounds so she can eventually forgive, and the third to pray and plan as she moves ahead.

Of course, we also have positive emotions—joy at a wedding, contentment around the dinner table with those we love, enthusiasm as we begin a new job. Those uplifting feelings tell us important things too.

All of our emotions are gifts from God to help us process *everything* we experience.

Emotions are also a big part of what makes you amazing. They allow you to respond to life in deeply personal ways. They connect you with others. They reflect your awesome Maker.

—*You're Already Amazing*, chapter 4

Question 1: What messages about emotions have you received from family, religion, culture, or other places? (Example: "Big girls don't cry.") If an answer doesn't come to you right away, finish this sentence: "Emotions are . . ." Then consider when and where you first heard what you wrote down.

Head or Heart

All of us have emotions, but depending on how we're physically wired and the environment we grow up in, some of us experience them more strongly than others. Use the following chart to figure out if you're more naturally "heart-driven" or "head-driven" by circling the option on each row that sounds like you *more often*:

○ I prefer facts	○ I prefer feelings
○ People are more likely to describe me as logical.	○ People are more likely to describe me as emotional.
○ When someone expresses a strong emotion, I often want to withdraw.	○ When someone expresses a strong emotion, I often try to find a way to engage with them.
○ In conversation, I most often say, "I think . . ."	○ In conversation, I most often say, "I feel . . ."
○ I agree more with this statement: "Use your head."	○ I agree more with this statement: "Follow your heart."
○ I grow in my relationship with God most by learning a new truth about him and applying it practically.	○ I grow in my relationship with God most by experiencing him in an intimate way through a personal situation.
○ I find it fairly simple to compartmentalize my life. I can think about one thing at a time.	○ I find it difficult to compartmentalize my life. How I feel affects every area.
○ This is one of my favorite verses: "Do not conform to the pattern of this world, but be transformed by the renewing of your mind" (Rom. 12:2).	○ This is one of my favorite verses: "Trust in the LORD with all your heart and lean not on your own understanding" (Prov. 3:5).

None of us use just our heads or just our hearts. And that's the way God designed it—we're to love him with our hearts *and* minds. The purpose of the exercise is simply to help you understand which way you naturally tend to lean, because it impacts your life, makes you vulnerable in certain ways, and can also be the source of many of your strengths. As we move forward, we'll talk more about who you are emotionally and how you can use that to serve God and others.

✳ **Question 2:** Are you dominated more by your head or heart? Look back to the descriptions about both and write a few phrases that sound most like you.

_____

_____

Tip: Teenage Emma describes her school day at the dinner table. Her parents have a lot to say in reply, and they accidentally interrupt each other as they begin. Emma's dad jumps right in with, "I think that . . . ," while her mom offers, "I feel like. . . ." They've both just given her a shortcut way to tell which parent is dominated by his head and which is led by her heart.

If you want to know which way you or someone else is probably wired, listen to the verbs in your conversations. "Head" people use words like _think_ more often, while "heart" people usually gravitate toward words like _feel_. And yes, more men statistically fall into the "head" category, but women can definitely belong there too. While most people lean one way or the other, you may also find yourself or someone else equally balanced between "head" and "heart."

Expressing Our Emotions

Genetics play a role in how "emotional" we are, but so do the families we grew up in. Every family is a mini-culture that has its own version of what's "normal" and acceptable. We're often so used to how our families operate that we don't even stop to think about what they've taught us about emotions and how to express them.

Taking time to do so isn't about putting labels of "good" or "bad" on our family's emotional style. Instead it simply lets us recognize the reality of the environment we grew up in and then either continue the patterns we learned there or decide we're ready for a change.

Families and Emotions

Read the descriptions, then circle or highlight the title (Stuffers, Screamers, Surfers) of the one that reminds you most of your family.

Stuffers:

These families like to keep emotions where they seem safest—on the inside. Have a bad day? Keep it to yourself. Have a really big accomplishment? Settle down. Home is a safe, peaceful place. Please don't rock the boat.

Wardrobe item: A sturdy, all-season raincoat

Screamers:

The neighbors already know if you're in a family of screamers. Emotion? Bring it on. Or better yet—bring it out. Emotions are made to be expressed, not suppressed. Conflict is present and passionate. So is making up. When it comes to emotion, these families are loud and proud.

Wardrobe item: A bright, bold purse that holds a lot

Surfers:

If you're in a family of surfers, everyone just rides the waves. Low tide, feeling a little sad? That's okay—we'll hang out down there with you. High tide, everything fantastic? We can get up to that place and share the joy too. Conflict ebbs and flows naturally. Emotions are just part of life.

Wardrobe item: A pair of shoes that can handle it all—wet or dry

Of course, these descriptions are intended to be lighthearted. They're also stereotypes, so no family fits neatly into one or the other. What's important is recognizing that every family does approach emotion in certain ways that teach us about how we "should" engage with emotion too. Sometimes that's really helpful. Other times it leads us astray.

Question 3: Which description sounds most like your family? What did you learn about emotions from the environment you grew up in? Now that you're older, which lessons would you like to keep and which would you like to replace with new truth?

_____

_____

_____

Your *Life Coach*

When I walked across the stage to graduate with a master's degree in counseling, I felt like a toolbox rather than a diploma would have been a more proper reflection of what I was taking with me. One of the most powerful tools I learned to use was a simple question: "What makes this make sense?" In other words, "What might explain this behavior?" My professors encouraged us to ask it every time we worked with clients, especially families.

People make the choices they do for a reason, and when we can begin to grasp that, it takes us to a deeper level of understanding. That question also turns us into detectives looking for clues rather than interrogators demanding answers. If you begin to feel frustrated or confused by the way your family acted when you were growing up, try asking, "What makes this make sense?"

Whatever answer you discover doesn't minimize or dismiss any wrongdoing—it simply gives more perspective. Another phrase we were taught to remember was, "An explanation is not an excuse." In other words, just because we discover why someone chose to do something doesn't mean those actions were justified. But it does help bring insight, and once we can clearly see, we can ask God how he wants us to respond to the reality in front of us.

Emotional Style

Our family's emotional style, our life circumstances, and the way God has wired us are all factors in which emotions we feel comfortable with and which we'd like to avoid. Circle or highlight three emotions that are easy for you to express, and draw a line through three you'd rather avoid.

Afraid	Ecstatic	Jealous
Amused	Embarrassed	Joyful
Angry	Empty	Lazy
Annoyed	Encouraged	Lonely
Anxious	Enraged	Loved
Ashamed	Enthusiastic	Mad
Blessed	Envious	Overwhelmed
Bold	Excited	Peaceful
Bored	Exhausted	Pressured
Brave	Fearful	Protected
Broken	Foolish	Quiet
Calm	Forgiven	Sad
Cautious	Free	Satisfied
Certain	Frightened	Scared
Cheerful	Frustrated	Shocked
Comfortable	Fulfilled	Shy
Compassionate	Furious	Silly
Competent	Giddy	Strong
Confident	Glad	Supported
Confused	Grateful	Surprised

○ Content	○ Grieved	○ Suspicious
○ Courageous	○ Guilty	○ Sympathetic
○ Defensive	○ Happy	○ Timid
○ Delighted	○ Hopeful	○ Understood
○ Depressed	○ Humble	○ Valued
○ Determined	○ Hurt	○ Weary
○ Disgusted	○ Hysterical	

Tip: One of my graduate school professors, Gary Oliver, liked to say, "If you bury an emotion, you bury it alive."[2] In other words, it will resurrect itself at some point—often at the worst possible moment. If you're going through this LifeGrowth Guide and painful emotions come up for you, try to respect them, even if you've ignored them in the past. Share what you're feeling with someone you trust, and consider connecting with a counselor who has been trained to help women experience true emotional healing.

Obeying God instead of Our Emotions

Question 4: Read the story of Joshua and Caleb in Numbers 14:1–9. They chose faith over feelings and were the only ones to see the Promised Land. What's one thing they did that you can apply to your life?

While every part of the armor of God in Ephesians 6:10–17 is important, one stands out among the rest as we talk about emotions: the breastplate of righteousness. That's because it's the one that covers the heart. And that's really what we've been talking about all along. "Above all else, guard your heart, for everything you do flows from it" (Prov. 4:23). All of this talk about emotions matters because our hearts affect *every other part of who we are and what we do.*

At first I didn't understand why righteousness would be what covers our hearts. But then it became clear: *choosing to do what is right in spite of our emotions protects us.* Think of times in your life when you've let your emotions get the best of you. I'm recalling some now, and the first word that comes to mind is "ouch." Exactly. When we let our emotions get out of control, we get hurt. And often others do too. When God says, "Obey me rather than your emotions," he's really looking out for our best interests.

But it seems like a tall order, doesn't it? Choosing what's right regardless of how we feel is no easy task (at least for me—maybe I'm the only one). So I dug a little deeper into this idea of guarding our hearts, and that brought me to this Scripture: "Do not be anxious about anything, but in every situation, by prayer and petition, with thanksgiving, present your requests to God. And the peace of God, which transcends all understanding, *will guard your hearts* and your minds in Christ Jesus" (Phil. 4:6–7).

—*You're Already Amazing*, chapter 4

Question 5: Let's practice bringing our emotions and what's true together.

Emotion women often feel (example: insecure):

....

....

Message this emotion sends to our hearts (example: We're not good enough):

_____

_____

What God says is true (example: We are fearfully and wonderfully made):

_____

_____

What God wants us to do based on that truth instead of what we feel (example: Use our strengths and skills to serve others instead of holding back out of fear):

_____

_____

Tip: Everyone experiences difficult emotions, but if you feel completely stuck or overwhelmed, there may be a deeper issue. Depression can paralyze our minds so that even when we try to grasp what's true, we can't seem to hold on to it. Hope and joy are always just out of reach. Other symptoms of depression include:

- consistent sad, anxious, or "empty" feelings
- pessimism or irritability
- feelings of guilt or worthlessness
- loss of interest in people and activities
- tiring easily and often
- difficulty concentrating or making decisions
- changes in sleeping or eating habits
- thoughts of death or suicide

I've personally struggled with depression, and so have many other people who love God, including biblical heroes like King David and current Christian leaders like Sheila Walsh. Depression isn't a spiritual failure; it's a treatable condition. If you're experiencing several of the symptoms listed, it's time to reach out for help by contacting a counselor or your doctor. Your life is valuable, and you don't have to fight this battle on your own anymore. You've tried to be strong long enough, brave girl.

As long as we live in this fallen, broken world, we will hear lies that try to distract us from what's true. They may come from the world around us or from the emotions within us. Whatever the source, God wants to replace them with what our hearts really need to hear. He invites us to let his voice be the loudest of all. Can you hear him whispering words of love to you today? He'll remind you of who you are and who you're becoming as often as you need to hear it.

Your *Life Coach*

Anna approaches me shyly at the end of a conference. She stares at the carpet and confesses, "I know what's true, but I just don't *feel* it." I place a reassuring hand on her shoulder and invite her to sit down for a moment to talk. After asking her a few questions to make sure she's not struggling with depression, I begin to share about how our minds and emotions work when it comes to truth.

Like I touched on in *You're Already Amazing*, our brains make neural pathways when we think certain thoughts repeatedly. When we change those thoughts, it takes time for new pathways to form. And here's the kicker: while those new pathways are being created, what we know is right doesn't always feel true.

Many women start feeling guilty or getting discouraged at this point. Like Anna, they believe if they know the truth, then they should be able to emotionally experience it instantly. But updating a thought pattern is like learning a new habit, and it can take six months to a year for that process to be complete. The key is to continue repeating our new ways of thinking even though our emotions don't align with them yet.

If you know what's true and sometimes don't feel it, there's nothing wrong with you. You're not "less spiritual" than other people. You're not in trouble with God. You don't need to try harder. You're simply in the middle of being transformed by the renewing of your mind (see Rom. 12:2). Your Creator understands this because he's the One who made every part of you, including your amazing brain. God isn't demanding you feel a certain way—he's asking you to just keep believing and obey.

YOUR NEXT STEP: What's one truth or aha moment you got from this session? What's one way you'll use it in your life this week?

_____

_____

RESUME THE
SESSION 2
VIDEO
on your DVD
or online at
HolleyGerth.com
/amazing.

More LifeGrowth

Pick your favorite, do them all, or add your own.

Connect

Share what's on your heart after completing this session.

Blog: www.holleygerth.com
Facebook: Holley Gerth (author page)
Twitter: @HolleyGerth
Instagram: holleygerth
Pinterest: Holley Gerth
Hashtag: #alreadyamazing

Get Creative

Research has shown that there are six universal emotions: anger, fear, disgust, amusement, sadness, and surprise.[3] How we display those emotions shows up in facial expressions that are recognizable in even the most remote parts of the world.

—*You're Already Amazing*, chapter 4

Create or capture expressions of the six universal emotions as a reminder that *all* of our emotions are gifts from God. For example, you could draw simple faces, take silly photos of friends and family, or search for images online and print them. Put all the expressions on one of the blank Get Creative pages in the back of the LifeGrowth Guide or on separate pieces of paper, or make a digital collage with them.

If you're in a group that is doing these activities, be sure to bring your drawings or pictures with you when you meet for this session. If you shoot your own photos, tag me on Facebook or Instagram and use the hashtag #alreadyamazing.

Journal

Create a list of five to ten lies your heart often hears and the truth God wants to replace them with instead.

Example:

Lie—"I'm going to fail."
Truth—"I can do all this through him who gives me strength" (Phil. 4:13).

As I mentioned in the session, if you want help finding Scriptures, you can use a site like BibleGateway.com. Enter words or phrases in the search box, and it will give you related verses.

You can use the Notes and Journaling pages in the back of the Life-Growth Guide or your personal journal for your list of lies and truths.

Go Deeper

If you'd like more questions for group discussion or personal reflection, see the Go Deeper Guide included in *You're Already Amazing*. You can download a printable version at HolleyGerth.com/amazing.

Session 3

Our Amazing Journey with Jesus

START THE SESSION 3 VIDEO on your DVD or online at HolleyGerth.com /amazing.

Groups

Facilitators: See the outlines in the back of the book for recommendations on how to go through this session with your group.

Members: Review the work you've done so far and read chapter 5 of *You're Already Amazing*, then go through this session (except for watching the videos) on your own before you meet.

Introduction

I stare out the window of our plane at the vast expanse of blue water beneath me. There's nothing to give even a hint of our location. My husband points to a blinking dot on the flight-tracking app he has on his phone and says, "This is where we are right now." That little dot stays on course with us all the way to our arrival in the Dominican Republic.

I think of that dot again as we travel with Compassion International over the next few days and visit people living in poverty. In one tiny house, I glance at the single window and realize there's a word written on it: *Jesus*. I see the unexpected joy in the grandmother's eyes and know he has been taking care of them every step of the way.

The following week I go to a media conference. After days full of radio and television interviews about my latest book, I feel like hiding under the covers in my hotel room. And when I come home, that's exactly what I do as the flu knocks me out for a few days.

As I recover, I think about the contrasts I've experienced recently: Quiet and loud moments. In the spotlight and completely out of sight. Traveling far away and being stuck at home. I begin to feel a bit disoriented—like I did looking out that plane window.

But then it's as if God points to an unseen screen with a beating heart on it and whispers, "This is where you are right now." Oh yes, of course. He knows exactly where I've been, where I am, and where I'm heading. Somehow that lets me breathe easier and rest more deeply. After all, *you're not lost if someone knows where you are and is making sure you're going to get where you need to be.*

You may feel uncertain about where you are today. Maybe you have regrets about your past. You might feel unsettled about your current place in life. Or you could have questions about your future. No matter what, you can be sure of this: God loves you and knows your situation as well as location. He always has. He always will. His plan for your life is good, and he wants to guide you every step of the way.

O Lord, you have *examined my heart*
    and know everything about me.
You know when I sit down or stand up.
    You know my thoughts even when I'm far away.
You see me when I travel
    and when I rest at home.
You know everything I do.
                                    Psalm 139:1–3 NLT

Question 1: If someone asked you where you are in life right now, how would you describe it? (Example: I'm finishing high school, raising toddlers, or transitioning to retirement.)

What do you enjoy most about where you are in life?

What are the most challenging parts?

What is God teaching you in this place?

Your *Life Coach*

I stand in front of a group of women, and one boldly raises her hand. She clears her throat and announces what feels like a long-time-coming confession. "I love my family," she begins. "But I don't feel like I'm really living in my sweet spot when I'm being a mom." I see other heads nodding around the room, and I can hear the unspoken question, "Is that okay?"

Maybe you're wondering something similar. You've identified your strengths and skills. But there are important parts of your life where you don't always get to use those. I especially hear this from mamas who are in the thick of the diaper-changing, mess-cleaning, midnight-crying phase with young children.

Here's what it means to live in this world: there will be roles and assignments God calls you to *for a reason or a season* that don't totally fit who you are, and yet they must be done. And when we struggle with those, yes, it really is okay. It doesn't mean you don't love the people involved. It simply means the actions needed in that role or assignment don't come as naturally to you.

All of the roles we have in this life are *temporary*. Who God made you is *eternal*. A thousand years from now you will not be in the thick of motherhood or at a particular job. But you will still have your strengths and skills. Knowing who you are beyond your current circumstances can actually help you better serve those in front of you today. Because then you can remember that this is *an assignment and not your identity*.

If you are living outside of who you are and what you are doing is *optional*, then prayerfully consider eliminating or delegating that part of your life. But if it's *essential* (like mothering your children), then it's time to make a strategy.

- First, find ways to incorporate *who you are* into *where you are*. For example, a friend of mine left a creative company she loved to stay home with her two kids. She found herself missing her work and decided to intentionally do art projects with her children.
- Also give yourself permission to have a way to express who you are outside your relational roles. My friend eventually began taking on freelance design projects and believes doing so helps her stay energized as a mom.
- Most of all, fight the guilt you may feel at not being thrilled about every part of where you are right now. It's okay to feel frustrated. It's okay to wish you were doing something else. It's okay to sometimes long for the days to go by faster.

(These principles can also apply to other situations, like having a job you need but don't love, caring for aging parents who are ill, or completing a degree.)

Wherever you are today is not the final destination in your life journey. There is more ahead for you. You don't have to worry about "losing yourself" because your identity is secure in Jesus forever. How much time do you have to fully express who you're created to be? *Eternity*.

Life Timeline

The questions we started this session with are like looking at a map and finding a big X that says "You are here." Imagine that as you look at the map, you realize there are also small dashed lines showing where you've already been. You can see how far you've come in a new way. That's what I want the following exercise to be like for you. We're going to create a timeline of your life where you can write down the experiences that have influenced you most.

In the space provided or on a separate sheet of paper, draw a horizontal line, then place dots along it where significant events have occurred. Above each dot, write a very short description of the event. Before you begin your timeline, pause and ask God to help guide your thoughts as you reflect on your life. See the tools following this exercise if you'd like more guidance and tips.

Your timeline will look like this:

(If you run out of room, you can draw additional horizontal lines on the page.)

Expect this exercise to be one you wrestle with as you go through it. It's normal to feel unsure about what to include or even a little overwhelmed as you try to capture your life accurately. If you feel like you have too much to write down, limit yourself to fewer than ten events. Remind yourself that there is no "right" way to do this and the purpose is simply to start seeing a big-picture view of your journey and God's hand in it. If you feel the need to make your timeline "perfect," set a timer for fifteen minutes and stop when it goes off, even if you feel like you could add more. What you do will be enough for the goal we're trying to accomplish.

Tip: If your life includes painful events and you find yourself getting stuck or avoiding this exercise, it's okay to quickly draw symbols rather than writing out what happened. For example, you could put a ☺ or ☹. You don't need to feel pressure to relive or go deep into those experiences. If hurtful memories or regrets continue to come up after you complete this process, consider sharing them with a caring friend or a counselor.

Tip: If you're someone who's very detail oriented, then this tool may feel overwhelming because you want to capture *everything*. To help you choose highlights, think of life events on a scale of 1 to 10. A 1 would be totally insignificant (for example, a trip to the grocery store) and a 10 would be something that permanently changes your journey (for example, moving to a new state). For this exercise, only include events that would be a 10 as a starting place. Then if you'd like to go back and add more later, you're welcome to do so.

❊ *Question 2:* How can you see God's hand in your life as you look at your timeline?

Here's the good news: God has a journey for *your* life. It looks different than anyone else's. The road he's carved out for you is yours alone. It's always the road less traveled because you're the only one who is ever going to walk it. Oh, sure, he'll give you wonderful traveling companions to go with you. But don't let that fool you: that doesn't mean their paths are the same as yours—just that they're parallel for a time.

So if you've been feeling guilty that your path doesn't look like Spiritual Samantha's, then breathe a deep sigh of relief. Your GPS (God Positioning System) is going to get *you* exactly where you need to go. And he promises to be with you every step of the way.

With that said, there are some common stops along the way in our journeys. The Israelites experienced them too. Taking a closer look at those can help us accurately place our "You are here" dots and give us a better understanding of those places.

—*You're Already Amazing*, chapter 5

Go with God

Once we've looked back at where we've been, it's time to embrace the place we are now. When God brought the Israelites out of slavery in Egypt and led them through the desert to the Promised Land, he gave us a story we could look to for guidance in our own lives as well. We're going to evaluate where we are so that we can do what matters most: *go with God*.

Read the following descriptions of where you might be in different areas of your life (Egypt, Encamped, Setting Out, Promised Land) and then complete the interactive tools provided.

Egypt

An area of my life where I feel . . .

- in bondage
- out of control
- oppressed
- separated from God's presence

"And I have promised to bring you up out of your misery in Egypt into . . . a land flowing with milk and honey" (Exod. 3:17).

Encamped

An area in my life where . . .

- I'm waiting
- God may seem silent
- doors aren't opening for me to move forward
- I feel the need to rest or heal

"The LORD replied, 'My Presence will go with you, and I will give you rest'" (Exod. 33:14).

Setting Out

An area in my life where . . .

- I feel an urge to take the next step
- God seems to be speaking and guiding
- doors may be opening for me to move forward
- I'm sensing the need for change—even if it's hard or uncomfortable

"Have I not commanded you? Be strong and courageous. Do not be afraid; do not be discouraged, for the LORD your God will be with you wherever you go" (Josh. 1:9).

Promised Land

An area in my life where there is . . .

- a desire or prayer answered
- a sense of being where I belong
- renewed joy and anticipation
- passion to possess and defend what's been given to me

"When you have eaten and are satisfied, praise the LORD your God for the good land he has given you" (Deut. 8:10).

Areas of My Life

I feel like my relationship with God is here today:

___ Egypt

___ Encamped

___ Setting Out

___ Promised Land

I feel like most of my relationships with others are here today:

___ Egypt

___ Encamped

___ Setting Out

___ Promised Land

I feel like my relationship with myself is here today:

___ Egypt

___ Encamped

___ Setting Out

___ Promised Land

Optional: You can repeat this exercise with other areas of your life that you'd specifically like to focus on as well.

I feel like my (example: dream, family, career) _____
is here today:

___ Egypt

___ Encamped

___ Setting Out

___ Promised Land

I feel like my (example: dream, family, career) _____
is here today:

   ___ Egypt

   ___ Encamped

   ___ Setting Out

   ___ Promised Land

I feel like my (example: dream, family, career) _____
is here today:

   ___ Egypt

   ___ Encamped

   ___ Setting Out

   ___ Promised Land

To tie everything together, let's build a map of where you are in different areas of your life. Take a look back over your answers in each section of this chapter and use them to fill in this life map:

Egypt

Encamped

Setting Out

Promised Land

Responding to Changes in Our Journey

When God says it's time to move, we may have one of several different responses. Circle or highlight the one that sounds most like you as well as a few phrases that stand out to you in the description.

The Settler—"What? Set out? I'm quite content right here. I just got things the way I want them. You go ahead, and maybe I'll join you later. Change is pretty scary, after all."

Strengths: Good at maintaining security and peace. Willing to stay with something as long as it takes. Faithful and trustworthy.

Areas for growth: Tends to view change, even when it's from God, as negative. May get stuck in a rut and refuse to move forward.

The Explorer—"Bring on the change! I'll race you to the Promised Land. I may not be sure where I'm going, but I'm making good time. Life's an adventure and new is fun."

Strengths: Willing to take risks and go in a different direction. Moves forward and often helps others do so as well. Embraces and encourages change.

Areas for growth: Sometimes takes risks or tries new things for the experience rather than being led by God. May put tasks ahead of relationships for the sake of progress.

The Traveler—"I'm packed and ready to go. I feel a little uneasy, but I'm still willing to take the next step. We'll see what happens. Life is just as much about the journey along the way as it is the destination."

Strengths: Takes life in stride and tries to move at the pace of God and others. Flexible and adaptive. Interested in what is ahead but doesn't rush to get there.

Areas for growth: Sometimes can end up wandering longer than necessary. May be indecisive or too easily sidetracked by others.

We each play these roles at some point in our lives, but one is probably your natural tendency. And this is never more apparent than when God says, "It's time to set out!" By understanding how we normally respond to change, we can pause and be sure we're really doing what God wants and not just what's most comfortable for us.

Your *Life Coach*

During my training as a counselor, I learned about a concept called "homeostasis." That's a fancy term for saying that humans generally feel more comfortable when things stay the same. It's like our brains have a "thermostat" built into them that automatically tries to maintain the status quo. Overall, this helps us have stable lives, families, and societies. But it also means whenever change of any kind happens, we experience internal resistance as our brains try to get things back to the way they used to be. If you've ever tried to eat healthier or exercise, you know exactly what this feels like.

If we persist in the change we want to make, then finally our brain decides this must be the "new normal." At that point it begins to "reset" the thermostat, and we no longer feel as much resistance. (How long this takes will vary depending on the type and intensity of the change.) The key to change is persevering until that happens. In particular, it's essential to resist the guilt we tend to experience because we don't "feel" like doing what is right even though our will is set on changing. We need to remind ourselves the resistance we're experiencing is simply part of being human.

It's also helpful to remember everyone else in our lives has a "thermostat" within them too. So when we decide to change, we can expect those around us to be uncomfortable or afraid, especially at first. This really doesn't have anything to do with their support of us but is just a reaction to change in general. Instead of getting frustrated or feeling hurt, we can try to offer affirmation or more information that can help their brains know everything is going to be okay.

Adjusting your brain's thermostat and helping others do the same takes a lot of energy. In other words, it causes stress. This is true of *every* kind of change. When we don't realize this, we can be caught off guard when positive changes are hard. Getting married, having a baby, or being promoted are blessings *and* challenges. So are improvements to our lifestyle like eating healthier, exercising more, or setting boundaries on our time. If you're going through any kind of change in your life, then expect to feel fear or frustration, become tired at times, and question what's happening. All of those are simply part of the change process going on inside you as your brain recalibrates to a new normal.

As I looked at the story of the Israelites again, I wondered how they knew when to stay put and when to move along. It turns out the answer is right there in the middle of the story:

Whenever the cloud lifted from above the tent, the Israelites set out; wherever the cloud settled, the Israelites encamped. At the LORD's command the Israelites set out, and at his command they encamped. (Num. 9:17–18)

The cloud above the temple was God's presence. So to sum all that up, *wherever God went, the Israelites went too.* He asks us to do the same in our lives.

—*You're Already Amazing*, chapter 5

Question 3: Read Numbers 9:15–23 for more about how the Israelites knew when to stay and when to go. What does this story tell you about what matters most to God in the journey of our lives?

We can get focused on the "what" and "where" of our journey, but God is much more concerned about the "who." He wants to share our lives and keep us close to him every step of the way. Take a moment to tell God you're willing to go with him wherever he leads you.

God, my life is yours, and I will go wherever you want to lead me. I want you to know . . .

Question 4: While God does want us to surrender our future to him, he also desires for us to have hopes and dreams about what may be ahead. Write down one to three things you'd like to see God do in your life.

Tip: You may not have a specific dream or desire that came to mind, and that's okay. It may be easier to think in terms of a general direction. Asking yourself this question can help you do so: How would I like my life to be different a year from now?

We will *go* with God and NEVER let **anything** or *anyone* STOP US.

—HOLLEY GERTH

Your *Life Coach*

When I talk with people about their dreams and they ask, "But how do I know this is from God?" I usually point them to Romans 12:2, which says, "Do not conform to the pattern of this world, but be transformed by the renewing of your mind. Then you will be able to test and approve what God's will is—his good, pleasing, and perfect will."

In this verse, Paul tells us we are to "test and approve" God's will. In other words, we've gotta try stuff. We don't usually like that approach. It's scary. We might mess up. We could get it wrong. And yet that is the only way for us to really know God's will—by experiencing it.

The precursor to that process is to be transformed by the renewing of our minds. In other words, to be committed to seeing our lives from God's perspective. We do that first by being in his Word on a regular basis. The Bible is not a static text but rather is "alive and active" (Heb. 4:12) so God can use it to show us what we need for our daily lives.

If our dream means pursuing a new opportunity, we can also ask ourselves a series of questions that help us determine whether or not it's likely to be from God.

These ten questions from my devotional *Opening the Door to Your God-Sized Dream* can be helpful when evaluating a decision or dream:

- Does this fit with my strengths?
- Does this fit with my skills?
- Have my life experiences prepared me for it?
- What do the people I trust most say about it?
- Do I feel an inner tug or "leading" from God to do it?
- Does the opportunity line up with Scripture and what I understand to be God's purpose for me?

- Are there any possible "phantom reasons" that could be tempting me to say yes when God wants me to say no (e.g., fear, guilt, a desire to please people)?
- If I say yes, what will it mean saying no to?
- If I say no, what will it mean saying yes to?
- When I look back in ten years, will this be a story I want to share?

After evaluating and praying, it's time to "test and approve." In other words, you move forward with what God has asked you to do to the best of your knowledge. You stay closely connected to him in the process, and as you go, you adjust. If you make a mistake, you learn from it. If you clearly see his hand in something, you do more of it. God's will isn't something we see in full in one day. It's more often something we discover along the way.[4]

We'll talk even more about God's plan for your life and specific next steps you can take in the coming sessions. For now, remember God knows where you've been, where you are, and where you're going. He loves you and he will never leave you. There's nothing you will face that you can't overcome together. And one day you'll be Home forever.

Your Next Step: What's one truth or aha moment you got from this session? What's one way you'll use it in your life this week?

RESUME THE SESSION 3 VIDEO on your DVD or online at HolleyGerth.com /amazing.

More LifeGrowth

Pick your favorite, do them all, or add your own.

Connect

Share what's on your heart after completing this session.

Blog: www.holleygerth.com
Facebook: Holley Gerth (author page)
Twitter: @HolleyGerth
Instagram: holleygerth
Pinterest: Holley Gerth
Hashtag: #alreadyamazing

Get Creative

Use patterned paper, markers, stickers, or whatever you'd like to make another version of your life timeline that's colorful and reflects who you are.

You can put your timeline on one of the blank Get Creative pages in the back of the LifeGrowth Guide or use a separate piece of paper.

If you're in a group that is doing these activities, your facilitator will let you know if you should do this before you meet or if you'll complete this project together.

Journal

Sometimes we need permission to put our dreams and desires on paper. Take time today to write out your hopes as a prayer to God. This will probably feel scary—that's normal and just part of the process. Ask God to give you the courage to do it anyway.

You can use the Notes and Journaling pages in the back of the LifeGrowth Guide or your personal journal.

Go Deeper

If you'd like more questions for group discussion or personal reflection, see the Go Deeper Guide included in *You're Already Amazing*. You can download a printable version at HolleyGerth.com/amazing.

Session 4

God's Plan for Our Relationships

**START THE
SESSION 4
VIDEO**
on your DVD
or online at
HolleyGerth.com
/amazing.

Groups

Facilitators: See the outlines in the back of the book for recommendations on how to go through this session with your group.

Members: Read chapters 6 and 7 of *You're Already Amazing* and go through this session (except for watching the videos) on your own before you meet.

Introduction

Huguette Marcelle Clark inherited one of the largest fortunes in the history of America. Born in 1906, she lived to be over one hundred years old and owned several custom mansions filled with impressive art collections and beautiful antique furniture.

Yet here's the irony: although in good health, Huguette went decades without visiting her lavish residences, gazing at her exquisite paintings, sitting on her luxurious sofas, or even inviting others to do so. She eventually moved to a hospital room (even though she didn't need special care) and spent her final years in a tiny, bare space with one small window.[5]

Something made Huguette decide to hide who she was and what she had to offer. Although her story is unusual, I can relate to her in a way, and I imagine you can too. God creates us in amazing ways, and yet we often struggle with grasping the true value of who he's made us. So we keep the doors to our hearts shut and eventually assign our souls to a corner. Insecurity or fear of rejection keeps us alone. Without even meaning for it to happen, we let the world miss out on who we are, what we have to give, and the beauty God has placed within us.

I used to tell myself, "When I can just improve this part of who I am, then I'll let people into it." Have you ever said the same? Eventually I realized God wasn't asking for my life to be an "immaculate mansion" before I shared it with others. Instead, he was inviting me to embrace who I was right now, right here . . . with stains on the carpet, dirty dishes in the sink, and dust bunnies still hiding in the corners of my heart.

None of us are perfect. But we are all fearfully and wonderfully made. You are a one-of-a-kind creation by a divine designer. You're not meant for hiding or holding back. Instead, your purpose is to love and be loved. It's time to open the doors, pull back the curtains, and truly share who you are with the world.

As the daughters of Eve, being made to share life with others is especially true of us—it's central to what makes each of us amazing. God created Eve with relationships in mind. When we think of Eve being created as a "helper" for Adam (Gen. 2:18), we tend to assume that word describes her role. But what if it's much deeper than that? What if it describes her heart?

Think of the women in your life. Encouraging, comforting, cooking, painting, working . . . it's almost all for someone else. They labor on behalf of love. This "helping" varies in its intensity. Sometimes it's a soft hand brushed across the hot brow of a sick child. But often it's fierce, strong, wild, bold.

The word for "helper" is the same word often used when God helps us. David uses it in the Psalms: "We wait in hope for the LORD; he is our help and our shield" (33:20). Here the help that comes from God is the kind one needs in war—it stands side by side with a shield.

We, as women, often do go to battle. We fight cancer. We fight for our marriages. We fight for our children. And in doing so, we help. . . .

We are "helpers" created and called by the One who is our help. So we must look to him for the complete picture of what that word means. God's heart is the place where "woman" began, and though we may look elsewhere, it is still the place where we (as women) find who we are in the end.

—*You're Already Amazing*, chapter 6

Question 1: Our beliefs about who we are impact our relationships from a young age. What were you taught about women in your family, church, or culture as you were growing up? If it helps, use these prompts: "Women are . . ." and "Women are not . . ."

Question 2: Read Genesis 2:15–24. Pay special attention to verse 18—it's the first time in the creation story God says something is "not good." Why do you think God said that?

_____

_____

_____

Question 3: God describes Eve as a "helper" for Adam. The word is actually the same one used in other places in Scripture to describe how God helps us. With that in mind, how would you define what being a helper really means?

_____

_____

_____

Being Wise in Our Relationships

Adam lived in a perfect relationship with God, and yet his Creator still said that it was not good for him to be alone. Sometimes we tell ourselves, "God is all I need! I should be able to handle life on my own!" But that was never our Maker's intent. No matter how "spiritual" we are, we will need other people in our lives.

While God doesn't want us to avoid relationships, he does want us to be wise about who has access to our hearts. "Above all else, guard your heart, for everything you do flows from it" (Prov. 4:23). How do you know if someone in your life is safe? The short answer: if they love you the way God does.

∼ *Safe People* ∼

First Corinthians 13, often called "the love chapter," gives us a way to evaluate if the people in our lives are safe. As practice, think of someone in your life, then place a check mark by or highlight the description that fits this person most of the time for each line. If you want to grow in your relationships, also take a moment to think about how others would fill out this chart if they were thinking of you.

Safe Behavior	Unsafe Behavior
∘ Practices patience	∘ Frequently gets impatient
∘ Treats me with kindness	∘ Treats me unkindly
∘ Finds joy in my blessings and success	∘ Envies me
∘ Stays humble	∘ Is prideful
∘ Gives unselfishly	∘ Doesn't consider my needs or desires
∘ Is slow to become angry	∘ Quickly becomes angry
∘ Doesn't hold grudges	∘ Holds grudges
∘ Trusts me	∘ Is suspicious and untrusting
∘ Believes the best	∘ Believes the worst
∘ Sticks with me no matter what	∘ Abandons me when I need them most

Your *Life Coach*

You can't control or change anyone. But you can determine how you allow yourself to be treated. If someone is acting in unsafe ways toward you, then you can say, "I want to be in a relationship with you, but I will not tolerate this behavior. Please let me know when you're ready to speak or act differently." This is the way God treats us. He tells us that he unconditionally loves us and desires to be part of our lives. But he also makes it clear that if we choose to act in certain ways, it will put distance in our relationship with him. God has strong boundaries, and we can as well.

Note: If abuse of any kind is involved, remove yourself from danger immediately. Then seek help from someone trustworthy and equipped to help you determine what you need to do next, such as a counselor. No matter what your abuser may be telling you, *it's not your fault and it's not okay.*

Question 4: Who are the safe people in your life? What are some ways you can let them know you appreciate them?

_____

_____

_____

Releasing Control in Our Relationships

As women we're still impacted by that one important choice Eve made in the Garden. Ultimately, that choice was about control. Eve wanted to "be like God, knowing good and evil" (Gen. 3:5). While it may hurt to admit, many of us want the same—especially in relationships.

Control can usually be traced back to one emotion: fear. . . .

The reality is that life and relationships *aren't* completely safe. Jesus said, "In this world you will have trouble" (John 16:33). We will get hurt. We will face loss. We will be disappointed. It seems as if control is a cure for this—but it's only an illusion. It traps us tight within our fears. Freedom only comes when we find security in Jesus, when we realize that life is hard but he is good and *no matter what happens* he'll get us through it. Life is risk. Love is risk.

—*You're Already Amazing*, chapter 6

As we talked about in the previous section, we can choose how we let others treat us, but we can't control or change anyone else. Yet as women we're still often drawn to control as a way to make our hearts feel safer. There are two primary ways we tend to approach control as women. Both impact our lives and relationships. To determine which type of control you're drawn to most, place check marks by or highlight the descriptions that fit you:

List 1:

_____ I want to determine the behavior of others.

_____ I am often tempted to be critical.

_____ I may sometimes be seen as "bossy" or demanding.

_____ I have high expectations for those in my life.

_____ I feel unsafe in situations in which I can't determine the outcome.

_____ I'm drawn to positions of power.

List 2:

_____ I'm very strict with my own behavior.

_____ I'm quite hard on myself.

_____ I tend to be anxious and find it difficult to relax.

_____ I have high expectations of myself.

_____ I feel unsafe in situations in which I don't know what others expect.

_____ I'm continually pushing myself to do and be more.

If you had more check marks or highlights on the first list, you're drawn to external control. You feel safer when you feel like you can control the world around you and the people in it. If you have more on the second list, then you're more focused on internal control. That means you're likely to seek security by controlling yourself and your performance.

All of us struggle with control in both of these ways at times, but there's usually one tendency we're drawn to more than others. (I also want to be sure to clarify that this kind of self-control is different than what the Bible talks about. Self-control as a fruit of the Spirit is a natural outflow of God leading our lives. It's ultimately God-control. The kind of control we're talking about here is self-imposed so that we feel safe.) By understanding how we try to gain control in our lives, we can recognize those patterns and give control back to God so he can be our ultimate security.

Tip: When you begin displaying one of the behaviors in the lists you just went through, pause and ask yourself, "What am I afraid will happen if I'm not in control?" Then ask God to replace those fears with his truth and love. Even when we feel like we're in control, we're actually not. We can't take a single breath without God. Acknowledging that God alone is in control can help us loosen our grip and trust him with whatever we're facing.

Discovering How We Connect with Others

When we release control to God, we become free to express who we are in our relationships and to let others be who they're created to be as well. While all women reflect God's image, we do so in a variety of unique ways.

It's okay if you're not a "girly-girl" and don't relate to some of the traits typically associated with females. It's also fine if you're the princess type who loves anything that's pink and has ruffles or ribbons.

There's no one-size-fits-all description of how every woman is supposed to be. Celebrate and embrace your unique version of God-given femininity.

Imagine we're on a playground. One feisty little girl leads her peers in a spontaneous game. Another talks quietly with a friend in the sandbox. Both seem utterly content in the way they connect with others.

Then we grow up and learn words like *outgoing* and *shy*, and the labels make us squirm. When certain social situations make us feel uncomfortable, we tell ourselves we shouldn't feel that way. We pile on the guilt for not being "loving" and try harder. But the truth still remains—particular ways of connecting with others feel as natural now as they did back when we were those kids on the playground.

What if God made us that way? What if he wired our social tendencies just like he did our other strengths and skills? Perhaps the way you connect with those around you is just as needed as the other gifts in your life. Maybe it's even at the heart of what makes you amazing.

—*You're Already Amazing*, chapter 7

Your *Life Coach*

We're about to go through tools to help you discover more about who God created you to be. When women do these they often say, "I relate to several of the descriptions!" That's totally normal because none of these traits are absolute. We're simply looking for which one is your *strongest preference*. Ask yourself, "Given complete freedom to pick between all of these, which one would I probably choose *more often than the others*?"

Your Social Strengths

Setting

You have a dominant social setting preference. One way to recognize it is by asking yourself what you usually choose if you have an evening free to do anything you'd like with others. Do you plan a party? Have dinner with a few friends? Make time for a long chat over coffee with just one person? Your answer gives you a glimpse of who you are and how you relate to others.

Read the descriptions and circle or highlight the title of the one that sounds most like you. Then underline or highlight a few phrases you especially relate to in the description you chose.

One-to-One: You prefer situations in which you can focus intently on an individual. You listen carefully and seek to offer your full attention. Your conversations are likely to have depth, and you want to hear what's really going on in the other person's life and heart as well as share the same. While you enjoy people, you probably don't have the desire for an extensive inner circle. That would require spreading yourself too thin. After all, a relationship is a significant, serious investment that requires the best of you.

In a group of people, you may feel overwhelmed or frustrated that you can't give each person the attention you'd truly like. You also may have little patience for small talk and chatter, seeing them as a distraction from what matters most. You have a strong capacity to make people feel truly valued and heard.

One-to-Few: You are drawn to situations in which you can be in a close circle of people. Most often, those in that circle are people you already know. You feel safe and comfortable because you have history and an understanding of who is around you. You don't necessarily need to have deep conversations because you know so much about each other, although you can do so at times. You enjoy hearing how each person approaches life and learning from them. You also like seeing how each individual engages with the others in different ways. You are a peacemaker and relationship maintainer.

You don't necessarily mind meeting new people but don't naturally go out of your way to do so and may avoid situations completely if people you know aren't going to be there. You know how to talk as well as listen and can do so with one person or the whole group as the conversation flows. You make people feel comfortable and as if they belong.

One-to-Many: You thrive on groups of people. You have a seemingly endless capacity for connection. While others might be intimidated by having lots of people around, you are excited by the opportunity. You could be called a "social butterfly," and you often act much like one—flitting from person to person with ease.

Most of your conversations are more casual because you need to spread your emotional energy around, although you can go deeper if someone really needs you. If someone takes too much of your time, you may start feeling trapped. You're able to lead, speak in front of a group, or coordinate many people if needed. You love seeing how different people are, and there's no such thing as a stranger to you—just another friend waiting to be made. You make people feel included and help them engage in life and with each other.

Tip: If you're still having a hard time choosing one description, you can rank them instead (1 being most preferred, 2 being next preferred, and so on). You can do the same for the other sections that follow.

Structure

There are three primary relationship structures: leading, partnering, and following/serving. Depending on where you are (work, home, etc.), these may vary for you. But there's usually one that you naturally gravitate to more of the time. If you made graphs of each of these, they would look like this:

Leading	Partnering	Serving
You	You ⟷ Others	Others
Others		You

Read the descriptions and circle or highlight the title of the one that sounds most like you. Then underline or highlight a few phrases you especially relate to in the description you chose.

Leading: If you prefer the leading structure of relationship, then you're confident being in charge. You enjoy setting direction and inspiring others to join you on the journey. Those in your life likely listen to you and look to you for advice. When you're not depending on God as your ultimate leader, you may come across as controlling. But when you're being directed by him, you have the ability to take many people to places God wants them to go and to guide them well along the way.

Partnering: If you're drawn to the partnering structure of relationship, then you view everyone in life as your equal. You want to be side by side or face-to-face. You see connecting with others as an endless process of give-and-take. You care little for power but don't want to be taken advantage of either. You may become agitated by issues of balance and fairness. You have a strong capacity for coming alongside others and encouraging them, sometimes simply by your presence through whatever they face. You believe we're all better together.

Serving: If you fit closest with the serving structure of relationship, then you see humbling yourself as the best way to lift others up. You're willing to do whatever is needed and offer support without resentment or envy. You likely feel uncomfortable with the spotlight and avoid attention. You may sometimes use service as a way to make yourself feel needed or earn love rather than giving freely and confidently. If you find a worthy leader, you are quite content being a follower. You're a strong, steady support and gain joy from helping others in the journey of life.

Sight

When it comes to life, we all have vision that's stronger in particular areas. Just as our eyes can be nearsighted or farsighted, we see more clearly in certain social situations. In this case, it doesn't need to be corrected—it simply needs to be recognized and maximized. When you do so, your way of seeing the world can become a strength.

There are two primary types of sight when it comes to relationships: internal and external.

Read the descriptions and circle or highlight the title of the one that sounds most like you. Then underline or highlight a few phrases you especially relate to in the description you chose.

External: If your social sight is externally focused, then you're highly tuned in to your environment and the people in it. You notice details about the ones you love. You remember events in their lives like birthdays. You are aware of what's going on with them and take the time to show it. When you're in a conversation, you have the ability to watch facial expressions and body language while staying aware of your surroundings too. You're likely to ask "How's it going?" and really want to know what's happening in the lives of others. You show love in tangible, often practical ways. You're more likely to be an extrovert.

Internal: If your social sight is internally focused, then you are highly tuned in to the unseen world that exists around you and within those you love. You seem to intuitively understand what others are feeling or thinking, often without them telling you so. You are more likely to live in the realm of the heart. When you talk intently with someone, the rest of the room frequently fades away. You want to know the passions, desires, and dreams of those you love. You express that you care in ways that are invisible but still deeply meaningful—listening, speaking encouraging words, and silently providing support. You're more likely to be an introvert.

Sphere of Needs

When you use your social sight to focus on others, needs begin to appear. And of course you want to meet them. The needs that stand out most to you and the ways you feel compelled to fill them for others are the final aspect of your social strengths.

Read the descriptions and circle or highlight the title of the one that sounds most like you. Then underline or highlight a few phrases you especially relate to in the description you chose.

Practical: If you're drawn to meet the practical needs of others, you're likely to see what needs to be done and then do it. You use your hands to meet needs—whether that is cooking, setting up, writing a check, or making something happen in a tangible way. You feel satisfied when you see actual results from your giving.

Emotional: If you're wired to meet the emotional needs of others, you offer your heart first. You know when someone is hurting or desires to have someone rejoice with them. You give through intangible ways most often—comforting, encouraging, bringing hope. You don't need to see actual physical results from the way you give other than a smile appearing or a tear being wiped away.

Relational: If you desire to meet the relational needs of others, then you see your presence as the best gift you can offer. You show up whenever it matters most—in the hard times as well as the happy. You may not even talk about what the other person is feeling or be compelled to take a specific action. You simply want to be there for support, to share the experience, and to be a connector.

Intellectual: If you focus on the intellectual needs of others, you're likely to try to connect them to truth first. You might offer to pray for them right away, share a helpful Scripture, or pass along a book that offers wisdom for their situation. You want others in your life to know what matters most because you believe it impacts every area of their lives.

You may wonder why there isn't a category labeled "spiritual." That's because I believe all of these are spiritual. Jesus said if we even give a cup of cold water to someone in his name, it matters and will be rewarded (see Matt. 10:42).

Also, Jesus wants us as believers to meet all kinds of needs in the lives of others. This is intended not to get us off the hook for serving in other areas but instead to help us see where we're probably called to give more of the time. If you could only do one of the categories listed, which one would you pick? That's your primary sphere of needs, but stay open to serving in other ways as well.

Putting It All Together

Write your top choice for each of the previous sections.

Setting:

Structure:

Sight:

_____

Sphere of needs:

_____

⚜ **Question 5:** Describe a moment in your life recently when you felt like you were living in your social strengths and being a blessing. Where were you? What were you doing? Who was with you? How did you feel? Include as many details as you can.

_____

_____

_____

Tip: If answering question 5 made you realize you're spending a lot of time outside your social strengths on a consistent basis, then it may be time to pause and do some evaluating. Think of a role or social situation that's consistently draining for you, then ask yourself the following questions to see if any changes can be made:

- "Is this role or social situation truly necessary? Can it be eliminated?" If so, prayerfully consider how that can happen.
- If it cannot be eliminated, ask, "Can someone else take my place?" Sometimes we are right in the middle of a place God wants someone else to be. Stepping out of it is not selfish; it's service.
- If someone else can't take your place, ask, "Can I decrease the amount of time I spend in this role or social situation?" If so, begin making a plan to do so.
- If not, ask, "What or who will help strengthen and sustain me while I'm outside my social sweet spot?" Then take action to get the extra support you need. For example, I sometimes attend

I need *you.*

You need *me.*

God's kingdom needs *us.*

And we're better

together.

—Holley Gerth

Print or pass along this word art through the "Share the Love" section of HolleyGerth.com/amazing.

conferences as part of my job. My social strength is one-on-one, so I often ask someone who has a one-to-many strength to stick by me at those events. We get to have some great conversations when it's just the two of us, and I have backup when I need to engage with a group of people.

If you want more encouragement on this topic, look back to Session 3 where we talked about roles and assignments that don't totally fit with who we are.

The body is not made up of one part but of many. Now if the foot should say, "Because I am not a hand, I do not belong to the body," it would not for that reason stop being part of the body. And if the ear should say, "Because I am not an eye, I do not belong to the body," it would not for that reason stop being part of the body. If the whole body were an eye, where would the sense of hearing be? If the whole body were an ear, where would the sense of smell be? But in fact *God has placed the parts in the body,* every one of them, just as he wanted them to be. (1 Cor. 12:14–18)

Like we talked about earlier in this LifeGrowth Guide, research has shown that how much a woman thrives is impacted more by how much time she spends in her sweet spot than any other factor, and that sweet spot includes your social strengths. When you align with who God created you to be, everything changes. You're fully alive, others are blessed, and he is glorified.

Yes, serving others includes doing what's hard and stepping out of our comfort zones at times. *But denying ourselves doesn't mean denying who God made us.* "For we are God's masterpiece. He has created us anew in Christ Jesus, so we can do the good things he planned for us long ago" (Eph. 2:10 NLT).

And loving well is the best thing of all.

YOUR NEXT STEP: What's a truth or aha moment you're taking away from this session? What's one way you'll apply that in your life this week?

_____

_____

RESUME THE SESSION 4 VIDEO on your DVD or online at HolleyGerth.com /amazing.

MORE LIFEGROWTH

Pick your favorite, do them all, or add your own.

Connect

Share what's on your heart after completing this session.

Blog: www.holleygerth.com
Facebook: Holley Gerth (author page)
Twitter: @HolleyGerth
Instagram: holleygerth
Pinterest: Holley Gerth
Hashtag: #alreadyamazing

Get Creative

Plan a time to connect with others in a fun way. If you're doing the LifeGrowth Guide in a group, your facilitator will talk more with you about what your group will do.

I'd love for you to take some photos while you're together and share them with me on Facebook or Instagram. You can also include the hashtag #alreadyamazing.

Journal

One of the passages of Scripture we covered this week talks about how we're all part of the body of Christ. For example, if you're always reaching out to others, you might be a hand. If you like to speak up for those who are overlooked, you might be a mouth. If you're a quiet, sensitive connector, you might be a heart. Spend some time writing about the part of the body you think you are and asking God for insight on ways you can serve.

You can use the Notes and Journaling pages in the back of the LifeGrowth Guide or your personal journal.

Go Deeper

If you'd like more questions for group discussion or personal reflection, see the Go Deeper Guide included in *You're Already Amazing.* You can download a printable version at HolleyGerth.com/amazing.

Session 5

God's Purpose for Our Lives

Groups

Facilitators: See the outlines in the back of the book for recommendations on how to go through this session with your group.

Members: Read chapters 8 and 9 of *You're Already Amazing* and go through this session (except for watching the videos) on your own before you meet.

Introduction

She opens her door and invites me in with a smile followed by a warm hug. We sit down at the kitchen table, and she places a brightly colored plate in front of me. I study the pretty design around the edges. My college mentor, Beth English, doesn't believe in matching sets.

Every dish she owns is wonderfully unique, and I'm always intrigued to discover what I'll eat off each week. She has a knack for noticing the one-of-a-kind beauty in people too.

Beth asks how I'm doing, and I share about my endlessly busy schedule. After listening intently, Beth leans back and says words that will stay with me for decades to come: "Holley, the hardest choices in life aren't between bad and good. They're between good and best."

My wise mentor has recognized something in me that will take me much longer to see. I have a tendency to say yes to anything that looks appealing. With well-meaning intentions, I fill my calendar and heart beyond their capacities and then wonder why I spend so much time being exhausted.

Becoming a thriving adult requires discovering we have limits and then figuring out a filter that helps us choose what truly matters most. In today's world, there will always be plenty of choices. But not everything we *can* do is something we *should* do. Even if someone else really, really wants us to do it.

As the verse we ended Session 4 with said, "We are God's masterpiece. He has created us anew in Christ Jesus, so we can do the good things he planned for us long ago" (Eph. 2:10 NLT). This Scripture includes two important truths for where we're going next as well: God created us for a specific purpose, and he has a divine plan that can only be accomplished through us. It doesn't say, "You ended up in this world somehow, so just get up every day and see what happens." No, you are here for a reason and you are irreplaceable.

God wants you to take ownership of your life. He wants you to live proactively rather than reactively. There will always be someone who's willing to tell you who you should be and what you should do. But God doesn't want you to be like anyone but Jesus—and only he knows how your one wild and precious life is to be spent.

In this session we're going to make sure you have a strong, effective tool that will enable you to say yes and no clearly and confidently. Then we're going to look at what steps God may want you to take so you can walk away from our time together with not just inspiration but a practical, doable plan.

It's time to embrace the very best God has for you.

START THE SESSION 5 VIDEO on your DVD or online at HolleyGerth.com /amazing.

A Brief Review

In preparation for creating your LIFE statement, go back to Session 1 in this book and use it to fill in the following areas.

My top three strengths:

_____

_____

My top three skills:

_____

_____

Who I'm especially called to serve (optional):

_____

_____

Your LIFE Statement

Now it's time to combine everything you've learned into a LIFE statement. LIFE stands for "Love Is Faith Expressed" and is based on Galatians 5:6: "The only thing that counts is faith expressing itself through love." A LIFE statement serves three significant purposes:

First, *a LIFE statement is a filter for evaluating decisions and opportunities*. While there will be exceptions, most of the time what we choose to do should fit with who we are and what we feel called to do.

Second, *a LIFE statement is intended to be an affirmation of what we're already doing*. On the days when our lives feel ordinary and we wonder if we should be doing something else, we can know, "Yes, I'm where I'm supposed to be and it matters."

Most of all, *a LIFE statement keeps us on track with what Jesus says matters most*: "'Love the Lord your God with all your heart and with all your soul and with all your mind.' This is the first and greatest commandment. And the second is like it: 'Love your neighbor as yourself'" (Matt. 22:37–39).

You can create your LIFE statement using the following process. (You may want to use a pencil for this section.)

Start with the common foundation we all share of expressing our faith through love:

I am created and called to express my faith through love . . .

Then finish that statement with your unique way of doing so in the world. The words you use here will likely come from your strengths, your skills, and who you're called to serve, which is why we've focused so much on them.

. . . especially by (verb ending in "ing") + (what) + (who) + (how)

Here's my LIFE statement:

I am created and called to express my faith through love,

especially by bringing <u>hope and encouragement</u>
(what)
<u>to the hearts of women</u> <u>through words.</u>
(who) *(how)*

Another one might be:

I am created and called to express my faith through love,

especially by <u>meeting the practical needs</u> of
(what)
<u>my family, friends, and community</u> <u>through service.</u>
(who) *(how)*

Here are some additional examples from readers of my blog:

I am created and called to express my faith through love, especially by bringing . . .

- the love and hope of Christ to hurting friends and strangers through spontaneous, God-inspired acts of service. (Valerie)
- leadership and creativity to my sphere of influence by caring for those God places in my care. (Amy)
- connection and covenant friendship to women through the spoken and written word. (Cari)
- comfort to those in any trouble with the comfort I have received from God. (Melissa)
- faithful service to my family by caring for their needs the way Christ wants. (Tammy)

Try writing your LIFE statement here (this is just a start—you can think and pray about it more later). If you want more help before creating your LIFE statement, see the additional guidance below this exercise.

I am created and called to express my faith through love, especially by

_____

_____

(verb ending in "ing") + (*what*) + (*who*) + (*how*)

If you're not sure what verb to use, "bringing" is a general one that works with most statements. Then look to your strengths, your skills, and who you're called to serve for inspiration to fill in the rest of the sentence.

You can also use the following questions to brainstorm what to put in each spot:

What—What is the noun form of my top strength? (Ex: Encouraging = encouragement, Supporting = support, Organizing = organization.) Just choose one strength to keep it simple for now—you can add more later if you'd like.

Who—Who will be helped by this strength? (Ex: family, friends, whoever God puts in my path.) If you don't have a specific answer to put here, just say " others."

How—How will I actually live this out? (Ex: caring for practical needs, leading with love.)

Now return to the space provided above and plug in your answers in the appropriate places. Add any connecting words needed for your answers to form a complete sentence (Ex: to, for, through).

As you've seen, my LIFE statement doesn't fit the brainstorming exercise exactly. That's because I used those questions as a starting place, wrote down my answers, and then tweaked the sentence to feel more like what I really wanted to express. The LIFE statement examples from my readers are the same way. As much as I'd like to provide one, there's not a "one size fits all" formula that will work perfectly for everyone. We're just too amazingly different!

The goal for this exercise is to provide you with the pieces you need to write a rough draft. Then you can use what you have to make something that's truly your own. The structure I've provided is just a suggestion. You can write your LIFE statement any way you'd like. It can be shorter, longer, or in an entirely different format. *There is no wrong way to do this*. What matters is that you're being proactive and intentional and seeking God in the process.

Tip: When I help women create their LIFE statements, they sometimes try to put everything they do into it and become overwhelmed. So I explain that their LIFE statement is like the hub of a wheel and the many ways they express it are like spokes. A LIFE statement doesn't need to include all the spokes, because they will naturally come from it. Then I draw an example like this to illustrate:

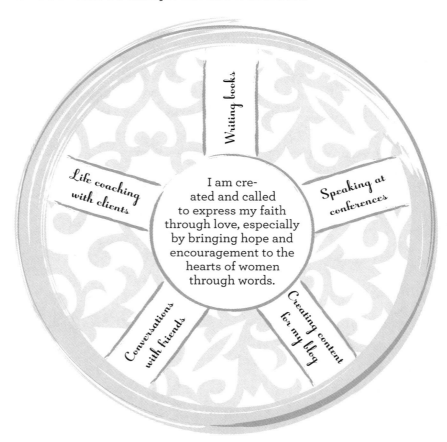

You can try creating your own wheel here. If you already have a LIFE statement, write it in the hub and then add the spokes. If you're still coming up with your LIFE statement, write down activities that feel like part of God's purpose for you on the spokes. Then look for what they all have in common to help you create your statement.

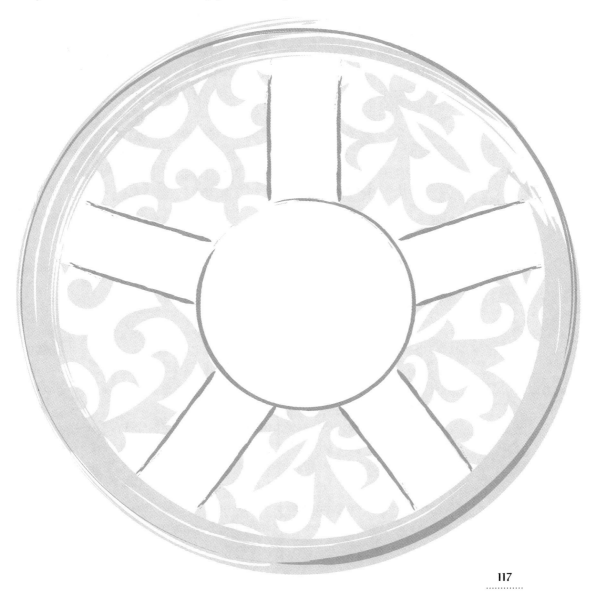

Tip: My LIFE statement doesn't specifically state all my roles or relationships. I see those as being part of the phrase "express my faith through love." My marriage, family, friendships, and personal walk with God are included in those words for me, and I know I'm going to focus on them no matter what. I need a LIFE statement that will remind me of my unique calling because that's what I'm likely to get distracted from most often. You can choose to go into more detail about your roles and relationships in your LIFE statement than I did, but you don't need to feel pressure to do so.

Some people also like to write multiple LIFE Statements rather than covering everything in one. For example, you could do a statement for your personal life and another for work. If that thought stresses you out, completely ignore this idea. If it appeals to you, pick one area to create a LIFE statement for during this session, then go back and add the others later.

Your *Life Coach*

If you're wrestling with your LIFE statement, know that's totally normal. This process often takes a lot of thought and prayer. If you get stuck, ask someone you trust and who knows you well to help you work through it.

The goal for now is simply to get something on paper. I've talked to many women who start with what comes to mind first, and then in the days or weeks to come they have an aha moment that leads them to revise their statement. The point for now is to begin intentionally thinking about your life purpose and begin putting words to it.

I also find that many women who struggle to put their LIFE statement into words are the ones who turn out to be living it most consistently.

It's so much of their "normal" that they don't even recognize it at first. So if you're feeling unsure, be gentle with yourself: it's likely you are already in the center of God's purpose for you.

Question 1: How have you lived out your LIFE statement in the past? How are you doing so now, and how would you like to in the future?

_____

_____

_____

Getting Free from Expectations

We know what God wants us to do, and we even have his power to do it, but it's still hard to consistently say yes to his calling on our lives. That's often because so many other voices (real or imagined) are demanding our attention as well—telling us what "should" be done.

All those voices we hear have one name: *expectations.*

We have expectations *for* ourselves.

We have expectations *from* others.

As I prayed about this section and what God wanted me to share, I asked him to give me his perspective on expectations. The surprising discovery:

Expectations are laws we place on ourselves and each other....

What's God's answer to those expectations, to those laws we create for ourselves or let others lay down for us? *Grace.*

—*You're Already Amazing,* chapter 8

Question 2: Let's take a look at the expectations women can feel. Try listing a few here. For example, women often believe, "I must say yes every time someone asks for help, or people will think I'm selfish."

I must _____ or this will happen:

_____

I must _____ or this will happen:

_____

I must _____ or this will happen:

_____

Now let's trade those expectations for grace. For example, "Even if I don't say yes to this request, I will still be loved by God and those who truly care about me."

Even if I don't _____ I will still

_____

Even if I don't _____ I will still

_____

Even if I don't _____ I will still

_____

Tip: If you're not sure what to write, think of the last time you felt insecure or afraid of letting someone down. There's usually an unspoken expectation lurking below those emotions.

Your *Life Coach*

Once we identify our LIFE statement and recognize the expectations distracting us from it, we're ready to make a plan for pursuing God's best for us. *This is the most dangerous point in our journey.* That's because all the work we've done on the inside is about to be expressed on the outside in new ways of living. And our flesh, the world around us, and the enemy of our souls would love for that to never happen.

If you start feeling distracted, overwhelmed, or afraid, then pause and simply ask God, "What's the next small step you want me to take?" Then move forward that little bit. The "Do What You Can Plan" we're about to complete will help you do so.

Creating Your "Do What You Can Plan"

Your "Do What You Can Plan" is intended to be exactly what it sounds like: a practical, doable way to take steps in the direction God is leading you to go. Our world tells us things like "Go big or go home." But I'm going to encourage you to think smaller.

Jesus said, "If you have faith as small as a mustard seed, you can say to this mountain, 'Move from here to there,' and it will move. Nothing will be impossible for you" (Matt. 17:20).

That's the secret: it's not about the size of our faith or the strength of our efforts. It's about who we're placing our faith in and what he can do. Nothing is more powerful than simple obedience.

The "Do What You Can Plan"

These principles and questions will prepare you to take your next step.

Small can be really big. What's one little step you can take to live out your LIFE statement this week?

_____

The meaning matters. Why is this step important to you?

_____

_____

Easy is not a four-letter word. How can you make taking this step easier?

_____

Slipups and setbacks happen. What is your plan for dealing with mistakes and mishaps?

_____

_____

Keep it sunny side up. How will you celebrate once you've taken this step?

_____

_____

Go the distance. What is the long-term goal this step supports?

_____

_____

Tip: Try to be as specific as possible with your next step, and always make sure there is an action associated with it. For example, instead of just saying, "Be more encouraging," say, "Send an encouraging note to Mandy by Friday." If you can't answer, "What will I actually do and how will I know when it's done?" then revise your step until you can.

Here's a shorter version of this process. Try using it for some other goals you have.

~ *My "Do What You Can Plan"* ~

I want to live out my LIFE statement by:	Small next step:	How I'll celebrate:
Encouraging others	*Send an encouraging note to Mandy by Friday*	*Get some fun cards so I'm ready for next time*

Your Approach to Change

We all handle making changes in our lives differently. Read the following descriptions, then place check marks by or highlight the lines that sound like you.

The Princess of Planning

____ You love order and structure.

____ You find great satisfaction in putting your thoughts in tangible form—whether that is in a planner, a digital calendar, or a list.

Yes, *Jesus* says we can do

ALL

THINGS

through him—

but he never says *we*

have to do it

ALL!

—HOLLEY GERTH

Print or pass along this word art through the "Share the Love" section of HolleyGerth.com/amazing.

_____ You want to know what's coming and be prepared.

_____ You enjoy details and can relax most when you know everything is in order.

_____ You like to think ahead and usually make time to do so.

_____ Others value your responsibility, conscientiousness, and consistency.

The Queen of Creativity

_____ You like variety and thrive on what's new.

_____ You have good intentions when you begin but often get bored with your goals before they're completed.

_____ You don't necessarily like details or feel compelled to keep track of your life in tangible ways like to-do lists.

_____ You like your options open. Too much order or planning feels restrictive.

_____ You're inspired by ideas, the intangible, beauty, and learning.

_____ You often care more about the process or journey than the result.

The Royal Highness of Relationships

_____ You believe life is all about connecting with others.

_____ You focus on who is in front of you, who is on the phone, or that email you just got that needs a response.

_____ Your schedule revolves around people, not plans or projects.

_____ When someone needs you, you often drop everything to make sure you can be there for them.

_____ You're the most motivated when you know what you do will help someone else.

_____ It feels like the direction of your life is often determined by those around you.

Add up your check marks or highlights to see which approach to change fits you most. Then review the following chart to find out more.

	The Princess of Planning	The Queen of Creativity	The Royal Highness of Relationships
Strengths	You get things done. You don't overlook details because you have them all recorded. You plan effectively and usually accomplish your goals.	Your creativity brings freshness and excitement to the world. Others enjoy you because you encourage and inspire them to see things in new ways.	You make people feel valued, loved, and important. You are friendly, open, and there whenever anyone needs a hand or just a hug.
Next steps for your "Do What You Can Plan"	Set aside time to create a concrete strategy for change. Write out what you want to accomplish and the steps to make it happen. Purchase or create whatever supplies you need to do so—a calendar, new journal, or chart—and put time in your schedule to pray and review your progress.	Get rid of the idea that you will find the perfect system and stay with it forever. Embrace your creativity when it comes to pursuing your goals. Remove structure except where it's absolutely necessary. Buy an unlined journal, put a whiteboard on the refrigerator, or start a notebook of ideas. Add variety to your plans so that your goal stays the same but the way you achieve it can change multiple times throughout the process.	Because you're so responsive to the needs of others, you may overlook your own. Begin to look at goals you might see as selfish (e.g., exercising) as an extension of the way you care for others (e.g., it gives you energy to play with your kids). You're not going to be motivated to do something unless you find a way it helps someone else too. So intentionally list that out with your goals and remember it. Also, whenever possible include others in accomplishing your goals by having them either join you in what you're doing or keep you accountable.
What to Watch Out For	Your goals becoming more important than your relationships with God and other people, being too hard on yourself, and becoming impatient when you don't see measurable results quickly.	Chasing after the new so much that you abandon worthy goals prematurely, giving in to boredom and quitting rather than finding a creative solution to push through it, and rebelling against all structure and order.	Abandoning your goals because they are different from the goals of others, listening to what people want you to do before you take time to ask God what he wants, and allowing others to put unrealistic demands on you that make it difficult to take care of yourself.

Tip: If you use tools like calendars, checklists, or journals, then make sure you're picking ones that fit well with how you're wired. For years I tried to use traditional to-do lists and notebooks with lined pages. Then a mentor challenged me to get rid of those and use an unlined journal where I could scribble and doodle. My pages may seem like a mess, but when I look at them I see order and an expression of what I want to capture. If the system you've been using isn't working for you, invent your own. You might love a very detailed planner or prefer a blank chalkboard. Whatever you'll use and enjoy is always the best choice.

Question 3: What are potential obstacles that could get in the way of the Do What You Can Plan steps you want to take? What are some ideas for how to deal with those? (Example: Obstacle—getting distracted; Idea—having a friend keep me accountable)

Potential Obstacle:

Idea:

Potential Obstacle:

Idea:

Potential Obstacle:

Idea:

As you begin to do what you can and live in grace, love will begin to grow even more in your life. With each choice you make, you become a little more of who God made you and draw a little closer to his purpose for your life. The LIFE that's yours to share with others becomes clearer. It's like the lines in the road keeping you on course.

Go out there and run the race he's got for you, girl. The world is watching and heaven is cheering you on (and I am too).

—*You're Already Amazing*, chapter 9

The most important thing you can do as you pursue God's purpose for your life is simply this: *don't quit*. There will be times when you feel discouraged or confused or wonder if you're headed in the right direction. That's just part of being human and living in this world. You can trust that God will get you where he wants you to go in the end. And remember, the journey of life isn't about how far you go . . . it's about who's with you. "God has said, 'Never will I leave you; never will I forsake you'" (Heb. 13:5).

 YOUR NEXT STEP: What's one truth or aha moment you got from this session? What's one way you'll use it in your life this week?

▶ **RESUME THE SESSION 5 VIDEO** on your DVD or online at HolleyGerth.com /amazing.

MORE LifeGrowth

Pick your favorite, do them all, or add your own.

Connect

Share what's on your heart after completing this session.

Blog: www.holleygerth.com
Facebook: Holley Gerth (author page)
Twitter: @HolleyGerth
Instagram: holleygerth
Pinterest: Holley Gerth
Hashtag: #alreadyamazing

Get Creative

It's important to keep your LIFE statement where you can see it every day. Create a fun version of it you can display and another one you can carry with you. For example, you might make small cards or bookmarks you can hang on your refrigerator and place in your purse.

If you're in a group that is doing these activities, your facilitator will let you know if you should do this before you meet or if you'll complete this project together.

You can also add your LIFE statement to the collage you created in the first session.

I'd love for you to take a photo of your LIFE statement and share it with me on Facebook or Instagram. You can also include the hashtag #alreadyamazing.

Journal

Record your LIFE statement at the top of a page, then spend time writing more about what it means to you and how you'd like to live it out, as well as sharing any questions or concerns with God. Ask him to guide you toward the plans and purpose he has for you.

You can use the Notes and Journaling pages in the back of the LifeGrowth Guide or your personal journal.

Go Deeper

If you'd like more questions for group discussion or personal reflection, see the Go Deeper Guide included in *You're Already Amazing*. You can download a printable version at HolleyGerth.com/amazing.

Session 6

How We Can Thrive for a Lifetime

Groups

Facilitators: See the outlines in the back of the book for recommendations on how to go through this session with your group.

Members: Read chapters 10 and 11 of *You're Already Amazing* and go through this session (except for watching the videos) on your own before you meet.

Introduction

I lean my head on Grandpa Hollie's shoulder and listen to the quiet in-and-out of his breath. Ever since I can remember, we've taken naps sitting side by side on his couch, but this time he's sleeping in a hospital

 START THE SESSION 6 VIDEO on your DVD or online at HolleyGerth.com /amazing.

bed. I pull out my phone to flip through pictures of us together and quietly whisper praise-filled prayers through my tears.

As I do so, an inexplicable feeling breaks through my sadness. The best way I can describe it is this: *fullness*. The glorious kind you experience when you push your chair back from the table after the most wonderful meal you've ever eaten and say, "It's so good, but I can't possibly fit in another bite!"

I didn't understand what that feeling meant at the time, but it comforted me and carried me as my grandpa peacefully slipped home to Jesus a few hours later. As I flipped through my Bible the next day, I came across a phrase that caught my attention. When someone godly passed away, they were often described as being "full of years" (Gen. 25:8). *Ah*, I thought, *that's what the fullness I experienced was all about*. It seemed God had somehow given me a glimpse of what my grandpa must have been experiencing as he pushed back from this life like a meal he'd relished and embraced his Savior face-to-face.

Jesus said, "I have come that they may have life, and have it to the full" (John 10:10). My grandpa is a testament to the truth of those words. His existence overflowed with love, joy, and meaningful work. He knew his strengths and embraced them. He used his personality and the ways God wired him to bless others. He remained fruitful and productive well into his nineties. And despite his longevity, the fullness of his life wasn't primarily about quantity of years but quality.

Our world tries to force us into busy schedules, endless to-do lists, and expectations that don't fit who we are. But simply having *a full life* and experiencing *life to the full* are two very different things. That's why this journey we've taken together matters so much. A purposeful existence never happens by accident. We must choose it every single day.

My prayer is that we intentionally savor the life Jesus offers us. Then we go Home to an even better feast and hear the words that matter most. The ones I'm sure my Grandpa Hollie heard. "Well done, good and faithful servant. . . . Come and share your master's happiness!" (Matt. 25:23).

P.S.: Here's a little behind-the-scenes blooper moment to lighten the mood: In the video for this week, I'm the one wearing workout clothes. After we finished filming, I went to change my outfit. Only then did I realize I had my pants on backwards. The entire time. Yep. I bet you didn't even notice, did you? We don't have to get it all right for everything to turn out okay in the end. *Whew.*

Question 1: Think forward to the end of your life. What legacy do you want to leave? How do you want to be remembered?

_____

_____

Life to the Full

Ironically, one of the biggest obstacles to living life to the full and finishing well is not taking care of ourselves. We don't want to be selfish, so we ignore our needs. Then we end up burned out, cynical, addicted, or just so exhausted we can no longer be effective. It's essential for us to learn to love ourselves just like we love God and others.

One way to shift our thinking about taking care of ourselves is picturing our hearts as internal bank accounts. Then we can make sure we're staying "full" rather than becoming overdrawn.

Certain things are like deposits: coffee with a friend, a long bubble bath, time spent praying. Others are withdrawals: an overwhelming project at work, a child with the flu, an especially busy season of life. We live in a fallen world, and there's never going to be a time when our emotional bank account always stays full. We don't need to feel guilty about it getting low sometimes. But we do need to be intentional about replenishing it so that we have something to give next time we're needed.

—*You're Already Amazing*, chapter 10

My Heart's Bank Account

Fill out the chart to begin getting an idea of what drains you and what fills you up.

Withdrawals	Deposits
(things that take emotional energy in my life right now)	(things that increase/restore emotional energy in my life right now)
Example: Conflict with a friend	*Example: Coffee with a friend*

Tip: If you're having trouble thinking of things, then fill in the blanks:

I feel the most drained after I _____

_____ . (withdrawals)

I feel the most energized after I _____

_____ . (deposits)

Everything we've talked about comes down to one thing: love. The end goal of taking care of ourselves isn't simply to be happy or personally satisfied. It's so that we can love God, others, and ourselves.

It's okay to take care of yourself, because you are someone's beloved. You are the bride of Christ. You belong to the One who hung the stars in place, who knows every detail of your day, who is waiting for the moment when you're finally together forever. You matter to him. He wants the best for you.

If you haven't figured it out yet: *you're amazing because you're God's creation and he lives in you.* You're valuable because you belong to him. You're worth investing in because he paid the ultimate price for you.

Dare to take the risk. Love yourself because he loves you.

—*You're Already Amazing*, chapter 10

Creating Your Personal Investment Plan

Spend some time brainstorming ways to be renewed. *These are not goals.* They shouldn't make you feel pressure or as if they are something you must do. These are deposits in your bank account—not withdrawals. For example, social might be "coffee with a friend" and physical might be "taking a walk on a nice afternoon to enjoy God's creation." Use the deposit list you made earlier in this chapter as a starting place and then add anything else that comes to mind. Take a few moments to ask God to show you how he made you and what you really need.

Here's an example to get you started:

Emotional—Watching a movie that makes me laugh

Mental—Reading a book I really enjoy

Physical—Walking the dog

Social—A "girls' night out" with friends

Spiritual—Writing a page in my prayer journal

Now fill up the chart below with more ideas for each area. You can use what you wrote in the "Deposits" column of the My Heart's Bank Account chart we completed earlier as a starting place.

Emotional	Mental	Physical	Social	Spiritual

While of course you won't be able to do each of these every day, you can return to this exercise and choose one when you need to be filled up. As a starting place, pick one you'll do this week.

I will make a deposit in my internal account this week by:

_____

_____

Date and time I will do it:

_____

Tip: If it still feels difficult to do something "for you," then think of what you would say to a dear friend who came to you worn out and weary. Imagine she shared, "I really need to be reenergized so I can continue to serve God and others. I want to (insert one of your ideas from the chart above here), but I feel really selfish about it." What would your response to her be? Whatever you would say to her is what you can say to yourself too. God loves all of us the same, and so being hard on ourselves hurts him just as much as if we were doing it to someone else.

Putting It All Together

Creating a plan for taking care of yourself so you can live and serve well for a lifetime was the final step in our journey together. We've come so far and you've worked so hard! I want to spend the rest of our time together looking back over all you've done and making sure you have everything you need to keep embracing who you are and moving toward God's best for you.

Let's start by doing a quick review of each session.

Session 1

Return to the very first question you answered: If you had coffee with a friend today and she asked how you were *really* doing, what would you say? How is your answer different than when you began this LifeGrowth Guide?

Session 2

Think of a time since you completed this session when your heart was tempted to believe a lie and/or you struggled with a difficult emotion. What helped you in that situation?

Session 3

Look back at your life timeline. Below or beside it, write your answer to the first question from Session 6 about your legacy and how you would like to be remembered. Are there any changes you need to make for that to happen? If so, what are they?

_____

_____

_____

Session 4

Review your social strengths by writing them below, and add an example of how you've used them since going through this session.

Setting:

_____

Structure:

_____

Sight:

_____

Sphere of needs:

_____

Situation where I've used these social strengths lately:

_____

_____

Session 5

Now that you've had time to think and pray about your LIFE statement, write a final version.

My LIFE statement is . . .

_____

_____

Because your LIFE statement is so essential to your moving forward with all we've covered in this LifeGrowth Guide, let's put some things in place that will help you stay on track with it.

∼ Emergency Plan ∼

Write down at least three ideas for what you will do when you face an obstacle or feel like you're getting pulled away from who God has created you to be and what he's called you to do in your LIFE statement.

When I get discouraged or distracted, I will . . . (Example: pause to pray, call a friend, read back over my answers in this LifeGrowth Guide.)

_____

_____

~ *Accountability* ~

None of us are meant to do life alone. Write down the name of someone you trust. Share your LIFE statement and some key truths God has shown you through this LifeGrowth Guide with that person. Then ask them to pray for you and encourage you as you continue your journey.

Name:

_____

What I will share:

_____

Date I shared:

_____

~ *Encouragement* ~

We also need to be able to remind ourselves of what's true. One of my favorite verses says, "David encouraged himself in the LORD" (1 Sam. 30:6 KJV). Write a note you can reread on days when you feel distracted from or discouraged about who you are and your LIFE statement.

Dear _____ ,

I want you to always remember

_____

_____

_____

_____

All we are, *everything*

God CREATED us to be,

becomes a *gift* when placed in his hands.

There's nothing he can't

MOLD, SHAPE, REDEEM,

Or FORM into something *beautiful.*

We don't have to be afraid or hold back—

we can just hold out our *hearts*

to the One who promises

to COMPLETE the *good work*

he's already started in us.

—HOLLEY GERTH

Print or pass along this word art through the "Share the Love" section of HolleyGerth.com/amazing.

Your *Life Coach*

Regularly reviewing what you've covered in this LifeGrowth Guide will help your life stay focused. I revisit what we covered in this book—especially my strengths, my skills, who I'm called to serve, and my LIFE statement—every six months to a year. That gives me a specific time to pause and pray so I can ask God if I'm moving forward in the ways he wants or if I need to do some adjusting. You might tweak your LIFE statement, add a new goal, or celebrate how far you've come.

Choose a day now when you'll look back through this LifeGrowth Guide. If you're in a group, plan a reunion so you can share an update with each other. Write the date and time just like you would for an important meeting. There are pages in the back of the LifeGrowth Guide you can use for recording your thoughts during your reviews.

Review date: _____

When you do a review, you can also ask yourself the following questions. As practice, answer them now, since we're looking back at our journey together. Note that these questions focus on what's going well. Research has shown that approach is much more effective in actually creating change in our lives than being negative or critical.

Question 2: How am I using my strengths and skills to love God and those around me? In other words, how am I already living out my LIFE statement?

_____

_____

Question 3: How am I taking care of myself so that I can continue to love well?

Question 4: How has God been showing me that he loves me? What can I be grateful for and praise him about right now?

I pray that you, *being rooted and established in love,* may have power, together with all the Lord's holy people, to grasp *how wide and long and high and deep* is the love of Christ, and to know this love that surpasses knowledge—that you may be filled to the measure of all the *fullness* of God. (Eph. 3:17–19)

You're already amazing because God made you, formed you, and lives within you. You're amazing because you belong to him, because he has a plan for your life, because with him there's nothing you can't do.

I hope our time together has given you some new tools, let God whisper some truths to your heart, and offered you some courage to take the next steps into all he has for you. But before we ever crossed paths, you had everything you need. You still do. You always will....

I know that you have what it takes to accomplish God's purpose for your life.

I know that the people whose paths you cross are going to be blessed because of you.

I know that your life is a story being written by an Author who has more in store for you than either of us can even imagine. Thank you for letting me share a few pages of it with you.

This isn't the end.

With the God who makes you amazing, it's always only the beginning.

—*You're Already Amazing*, chapter 11

▶ **RESUME THE SESSION 6 VIDEO** on your DVD or online at HolleyGerth.com /amazing.

MORE LIFEGROWTH

Pick your favorite, do them all, or add your own.

Connect

Share what's on your heart after completing this LifeGrowth Guide.

Blog: www.holleygerth.com
Facebook: Holley Gerth (author page)
Twitter: @HolleyGerth
Instagram: holleygerth
Pinterest: Holley Gerth
Hashtag: #alreadyamazing

Get Creative

Now that you've completed this journey, do some dreaming with God about how you can help other women embrace who they are and become all he created them to be. You can doodle or write ideas on one of the Get Creative pages in the back of the LifeGrowth Guide or use a separate piece of paper. You could also complete the collage you've created by adding a "Pay It Forward" piece that shares how you'll pass on what you've received.

My hope and prayer is that every woman who goes through this LifeGrowth Guide will then take at least one other person through it as well. You've done the work, and you're ready to pass along what you've received. You can do so one-on-one with a friend or family member, in a Facebook group, with your church, at your office, or any other way you'd like.

You'll find LifeGrowth Group facilitator guides for each session at the back of this book, and they'll give you everything you need to share this material with others.

Journal

Spend time praying for other women in your life who need to know God made them amazing. After you finish writing the prayers, consider sending one person a note saying you prayed for her and sharing some encouraging words.

You can use the Notes and Journaling pages in the back of the LifeGrowth Guide or your personal journal.

Go Deeper

If you'd like more questions for group discussion or personal reflection, see the Go Deeper Guide included in *You're Already Amazing*. You can download a printable version at HolleyGerth.com/amazing.

Notes and Journaling

Notes and Journaling

Notes and Journaling

Notes and Journaling

Notes and Journaling

Notes and Journaling

Notes and Journaling

Notes and Journaling

Get Creative

You can use the following blank pages for the Get Creative activities at the end of each session. You can also use this space for taking notes and journaling if you prefer unlined pages or run out of room in the previous section.

A few tips:

- Remember this is about a process and not a result. What you create doesn't need to be perfect, and there's no "right" way to do it. Give yourself permission to be messy and imperfect.
- Resist the urge to compare what you do with others or feel intimidated if you're in a group. Like we've talked about throughout this LifeGrowth Guide, we all have different strengths and skills.
- Pray as you create, and invite God to use this time to speak to your heart.
- From a practical standpoint, use what you have on hand as much as you can. Keep it simple and focus more on having fun than making it fancy.
- If your LifeGrowth Guide doesn't lay flat enough to work in easily, hold down the corners with something like paperweights or rocks. If your group is doing the activities together, bring these with you.

- If you use glue on your pages, your paperweights or rocks can hold your LifeGrowth Guide open until it's dry. If you need to take it with you when it's still wet, place it on the floor of your car with the page held open.

- Certain materials like heavy markers may bleed through the pages. If needed, place a piece of paper or cardboard behind the page while you're working on it.

- If you think of a different way you'd like to do the activity, go for it. This is all about creativity. Express who you are and do what you enjoy.

- If you're in a group, your facilitator will provide any specific instructions needed for each activity, like what supplies to bring with you.

Resources for LifeGrowth Group Facilitators

I'm so glad you're facilitating a LifeGrowth group! You've said a brave yes to what God has asked of you. You may be excited about what's ahead or a little nervous. Either way, I'm trusting God is going to work in powerful ways in and through you.

What You Need to Know Before You Get Started

- *You don't need to have it all together.* It's okay to be messy. It's okay to be unsure. It's okay to make mistakes. When you let other people see your imperfections, it gives them permission to be imperfect too. Doing so will help your group be a place of grace—which is essential for true growth.

- *You don't need to have all the answers.* If someone asks you a question and you're not sure how to respond, simply say, "I don't know. Let's try to figure it out together." This LifeGrowth Guide is about exploring, not explaining.

- *You do need to prepare.* This LifeGrowth Guide is personal, and women may be sharing in ways they never have before. By spending time not just answering the questions but really processing how the content applies to you and praying for your group, you'll make your heart ready to encourage others.

○ *You can change anything you want to about this LifeGrowth Guide.* Every group is different, so only you know what will truly work best for yours. You can add to, ignore, or adapt anything on these pages.

○ *You can't fail at facilitating.* There is no "right" way to do this LifeGrowth Guide. Release your expectations of your group as well as yourself. Ask God to accomplish his purposes through your time together and be open to where he leads you. *This LifeGrowth Guide is about growth and connection, not perfection.*

Who You Are as a Facilitator

The core message of *You're Already Amazing* is that God has created each of us in unique ways. So be who you are as a group facilitator. Whether you're an outgoing extrovert or a reflective introvert, you have strengths, skills, and a certain style of connecting with others that can benefit your group.

Try to avoid comparing yourself with others or doing what you think you "should" but isn't a good fit for you. Lean into who God has made you and ask him to empower you.

The most life-changing thing you can do as a facilitator is simply this: *love Jesus and your group.* Everything else is just details. If you start feeling overwhelmed, go back to this truth.

Also, make sure you have support during your time of being a facilitator. Ask at least one other person to be specifically praying for you and encouraging you. Pouring into others can be draining, so take extra good care of yourself and be intentional about staying filled up. That's not selfish; it's essential to service.

Practical Details

The Size of Your Group

This LifeGrowth Guide is highly interactive, and therefore discussion groups of six to eight are ideal. If you have a large number of women doing the LifeGrowth Guide, you can break them into smaller groups. Round tables work well for this, and it's recommended that you have no more than eight women at a table.

Plan to keep women at the same table for the entire time the group meets. Before the group begins, recruit one woman per table to be a co-facilitator. She will make sure the conversations at the table stay on track and be the designated person women at the table can turn to for extra help or questions (which can then be passed on to you if needed). You will facilitate a table as well. Ask your co-facilitators to go through the session outlines to prepare.

If you're meeting in a home or another setting where you can't break up a bigger group, explain to members that their answers to questions will need to be brief so everyone can share. If needed, find someone in the group to be the official timekeeper and ask that person to help you keep the group moving forward.

If it's not possible to have members sit in groups, brainstorm other ways to make the setting feel more intimate and how you can make time for each person to participate. For example, if rows of chairs are the only seating option you have, then you can ask women to form groups of two or three to answer questions.

When and How Long to Meet

The LifeGrowth Guide is intended to be completed in six sessions. Some groups like to add an extra meeting time before or after as a kickoff or wrap-up time.

You can meet every week, every other week, or once a month, depending on what works best for your group members.

Since the LifeGrowth Guide is highly interactive, the amount of time it takes to get through each session will vary based on the number of group members. Plan for sixty to ninety minutes. If you need it to be shorter, choose a few questions to focus on and skip the rest. If you need it to be longer, use questions from the Go Deeper Guide in *You're Already Amazing* for additional material. If you have co-facilitators, remember to communicate any changes in the session outlines to them.

Before Your First Group Meeting

1. *Invite people to be part of your group.* Depending on the setting of the group (church, work, your neighborhood), you can do this face-to-face, via email or Facebook, or through an official announcement. Choose what will best reach the women you have in mind.

2. *Create a way to communicate with the group members all at once.* An email list or Facebook group is usually simplest.

3. *Welcome the group.* Before the group starts, send them a welcome note and share any details they need to know, including:

   ◦ when, where, and how often the group will meet

   ◦ how long the group time will last and if child care and/or food will be provided

   ◦ what they'll need to bring each week: a copy of *You're Already Amazing* and the LifeGrowth Guide (both are available from online and local retailers, including at HolleyGerth.com/amazing), a Bible, a pen, and creative supplies (if you're doing the Get Creative activities from the More LifeGrowth sections together)

   ◦ Explain that the LifeGrowth Guide is highly interactive and completing the session work before the group meets will be essential because it requires time for personal reflection. Also let them know there will be questions where each person will be asked to share, and while they can always pass on doing so, you want them to be prepared.

4. *Be ready to refer.* You're a group facilitator. That means you're there to guide group members toward growth as well as help them connect with God, each other, and their own hearts. Women may come to the group with deeper needs than the group can address, and it's important to have resources you can refer them to if that's the case.

   Before the group begins, get the name and contact information of a reputable Christian counselor in your area so you can be ready to share it. Trying to meet all the needs in your group is impossible and unwise, and it will distract you from the ways you can truly be most helpful.

5. *Set boundaries that will make the group safe.* Sharing our lives with others can be intimidating and bring out insecurities in all of us. Making your group feel safe with each other is one of the most important parts of facilitating.

   Before your group starts or at the beginning of the first session, express that this will be a place of confidentiality, care, and encouragement. It's essential that you live out this commitment by encouraging group members during sessions and not letting gossip or criticism of others take place.

You may want to pass out copies of the following Commitment of Words and have each woman sign it (for a decorative, printable version, go to HolleyGerth.com/amazing).

A Commitment of Words

We commit to using our words to defend and heal, not to harm.

We will not gossip.

We will not belittle.

We will guard our sisters by always speaking the best about them, encouraging them into all God would have them to be, and offering grace instead of condemnation.

We will be loyal and loving, remembering that even if we disagree, we still fight on the same side—never against each other.

We will use our words to build up and not tear down, to bring hope and not hurt.

We offer our words as a powerful weapon to fight for each other on the side of all that is good, right, and true.

Session Outlines

Session 1: Who God Created Us to Be

1. *Welcome.* (If you're in a large group, the main facilitator will do this segment.) Tell group members a little bit about who you are and why you chose to facilitate this particular study. Review any necessary details, like how long the study will last and what they'll need to bring each week. Assure them that everything said in the group will be confidential, and share the Commitment of Words from the previous section if you're using it. Pray and give your time together to God. Watch Video 1:1.

2. *Introduction.* (If you're a co-facilitator, your role will begin here, and you will guide your table group through the rest of the material.) After the video ends, ask each person to share her name; whether she likes coffee, tea, or something else; and what she hopes to get out of the LifeGrowth Guide. Explain that each

person will need to keep what they share to a minute or less on every question so everyone has a chance to talk.

3. *Discussion.* Move to question 1 and ask your group, "How are you *really* doing?" Remind them that this is a safe place and they can freely share. Go in a circle to let everyone answer, but offer that if they don't want to respond, they can simply say, "Pass."

   Tip: Try to keep this lighthearted—you might want to come up with a funny phrase like "Pass the butter" that your group or table can use during your entire time together as code for "I'm not comfortable sharing that right now."

4. *Say the truth out loud.* Ask someone in your group to read Psalm 139:13–14 or do so yourself. Speaking Scripture is powerful, and it's an important part of this LifeGrowth Guide. Then discuss question 2 together.

5. *Strengths, skills, and service.* Take your group members through questions 3, 5, and 6 (question 4 is more for personal reflection). Have them share their strengths and skills by going in a circle. Then do open sharing for question 6.

   Tip: Sometimes women are uncomfortable talking about themselves. If you sense this, remind them that it's okay for it to feel awkward and that the point of what we're doing isn't focusing on ourselves but understanding who God made us so we can love him, others, and ourselves more.

6. *Next steps.* Give group members an opportunity to share a response to the "Your Next Step" prompt. Tell them they can also ask a question instead of responding to the prompt. If you have extra time left, spend it getting to know each other better.

7. *Watch Video 1:2.* About ten minutes before the group time is over, the main facilitator will share a few thoughts and play the closing video. When the video is done, the main facilitator will do whatever else is needed to wrap up the session (such as giving instructions for the following session, sharing prayer requests,

offering final encouraging words, transitioning to the Get Creative activity, etc.).

8. *Get creative.* If your group is doing the activity suggested in the More LifeGrowth section, there are two ways to do so. The first option is to transition to it at this point. Or you can instruct group members to start the craft at the beginning and work on it while you go through the session. If you're a co-facilitator, your main facilitator will let you know what to do.

Session 2: What's True No Matter How We Feel

1. *Welcome.* (If you're in a large group, the main facilitator will do this segment.) This session is about emotions and truth, so start by asking a question that eases group members into expressing themselves and helps the group personally connect. For example, "What was one of your highlights in the last week (or whatever amount of time it's been since you last met)?" If you have tables of women, tell them to do this as a table. When they're through sharing, open your time together in prayer, then watch Video 2:1.

2. *Identify the lies.* (If you're a co-facilitator, your role will begin here and you will guide your table group through the rest of the material.) After the video ends, read the lies and truths listed in the Identify the Lies section as a group.

   When the reading is finished, ask women to share the lies they added to the list. Because this can feel like a vulnerable question, share yours first. You may want to have two or three in case women aren't ready to open up. Remind the women that they'll need to keep what they share to a minute or less on every question so everyone has a chance to talk.

3. *Emotions.* Ask your group to share their answers to question 1. Have some examples ready. If you feel like getting creative, you might share a short clip of a song or movie that shows emotion. You could also print out a few quotes on emotions from

somewhere online like Pinterest. After question 1, move to questions 2 and 3.

Tip: Question 3 may evoke some strong responses. Try to guide group members away from talking negatively about their families. If someone begins berating their family or describing difficult events in detail, you can gently ask a question such as, "What would you like for your life to be like now instead of what you experienced then?" You might also pause and pray for the person. If needed, talk with them after the group meeting ends, and be ready to share contact information for a reputable Christian counselor (if you're a co-facilitator, your main facilitator should be able to give this information to you).

4. *Read Numbers 14:1–9.* Ask the group if someone would be willing to read that passage. If your group members don't always bring their Bibles, you can have those verses marked in yours, ready to read on a device, or printed out so you can hand it to someone. Then answer question 4 as a group.

5. *Practice the truth.* Discuss question 5 together. Go in a circle and have each person share her answer. Explain that we all experience similar emotions, so hearing everyone's responses will help the whole group. Again, remind your group that they can always pass if they're not comfortable sharing.

6. *Next steps.* As a wrap-up, give group members an opportunity to share a response to the "Your Next Step" prompt. Tell them they can also ask a question instead of responding to the prompt. If you have extra time left, spend it getting to know each other better.

7. *Watch Video 2:2.* About ten minutes before the group time is over, the main facilitator will share a few thoughts and play the closing video. When the video is done, the main facilitator will do whatever else is needed to wrap up the session (such as giving instructions for the following session, sharing prayer requests,

offering final encouraging words, transitioning to the Get Creative activity, etc.).

8. *Get creative.* If your group is doing the activity suggested in the More LifeGrowth section, then they should have their photos of the six universal emotions with them. Have a place where everyone can lay out their photos (you may need to use paperweights or rocks to hold the pages open if the images are in LifeGrowth Guides). Spend some time looking at them and talking about what you notice. Have fun and laugh!

   Encourage people to get their cameras out and take new photos as well. For example, take goofy pictures of your group making faces that represent each emotion. Maybe have a little contest where the silliest photo gets a prize at the end. I'd love to see pictures of your group! Tag me on Facebook or Instagram and use the hashtag #alreadyamazing.

Session 3: Our Amazing Journey with Jesus

1. *Welcome.* (If you're in a large group, the main facilitator will do this segment.) This session is all about God's plan for us and taking next steps with him. Express this to your group and explain that our lives are intended to be an amazing journey with Jesus. Ask members to share about one of their favorite trips or family vacations. Pray and commit your time together to God, then watch Video 3:1.

2. *Introduction.* (If you're a co-facilitator, your role will begin here and you will guide your table group through the rest of the material.) When the video is complete, have group members respond to question 1. This is a question where you could have everyone go around in a circle to answer and tell them they can pass if they don't want to share. Remind the women that they'll need to keep what they share to a minute or less on every question so everyone has a chance to talk.

3. *Timeline.* Transition to the timeline activity. Ask who would like to *briefly* share some highlights from their timelines. Be prepared to start by sharing yours. When timelines have been shared, follow up with question 2.

4. *Going with God.* Read the first paragraph under the Go with God heading. Then ask group members if they would like to share where they are in an area of their lives and what God has been doing in that place. You can also see if this activity brought up any questions for them. Transition to the Settler/Explorer/ Traveler tool and have a fun conversation by asking each person to share which one they circled.

5. *Moving forward.* Read Numbers 9:15–23 or have someone in the group do so. Complete question 3 by discussing it as a group. Transition to question 4 by talking about how it's okay to have hopes and dreams for our futures. Then give the group time to share answers to this question. Assure them it's okay if this feels scary or hard.

    Tip: The quote from *Opening the Door to Your God-Sized Dream* that follows these questions is intended to be a resource for those who want more on this topic. You can draw from it as a leader as well if you'd like to spend additional time here.

6. *Next steps.* As a wrap-up, give group members an opportunity to share a response to the "Your Next Step" prompt. Tell them they can also ask a question instead of responding to the prompt. If you have extra time left, spend it getting to know each other better.

7. *Watch Video 3:2.* About ten minutes before the group time is over, the main facilitator will share a few thoughts and play the closing video. When the video is done, the main facilitator will do whatever else is needed to wrap up the session (such as giving instructions for the following session, sharing prayer requests, offering final encouraging words, transitioning to the Get Creative activity, etc.).

8. *Get creative.* If your group is doing the timeline activity suggested in the More LifeGrowth section, you can transition to it now. Or you can begin it when you get to that part of the session and let members work on it while continuing to answer questions and go through the material. If you're a co-facilitator, your main facilitator will let you know what to do. The LifeGrowth Guide tells members to bring supplies with them, but you may want to have extra in case someone forgets or doesn't have any.

Session 4: God's Plan for Our Relationships

1. *Welcome.* (If you're in a large group, the main facilitator will do this segment.) Up to this point, the LifeGrowth Guide has been focused on each woman's personal journey. In this session we're transitioning to looking more closely at her relationships. To start moving the group in that direction, kick off with a prompt like "Tell us about one of your friends from childhood" or "Tell us about someone who has touched your life." Pray and commit your time together to God, then watch Video 4:1.

   Tip: The questions in this session are deeper than some of the others, so don't be afraid to go slower. What matters most for this topic isn't the amount of progress your group makes but instead how much they connect with each other.

2. *Introduction.* (If you're a co-facilitator, your role will begin here and you will guide your table group through the rest of the material.) Start by reading the quote from *You're Already Amazing* that begins with "As the daughters of Eve. . . ." Ask group members to underline or highlight phrases that stand out to them as it's read.

3. *Who we are as women.* Answer questions 1 through 3 together. Remind the women that they'll need to keep what they share to a minute or less on every question so everyone has a chance to talk.

Tip: The role of women can bring up conflict because people have different ideas about what that means. Try to steer your group away from taking specific positions (example: women should/shouldn't work outside the home) and instead focus on what's true of all women (example: we are highly valued by God and have a lot to offer him as well as others).

4. *Being wise in our relationships.* Share that because women are so relational, connecting with others includes many rewards as well as risks. Ask the group if someone would like to give an example of a person who fits the Safe Person list (question 4).

5. *Social strengths.* Explain that when we understand who we are and how we can love well, it helps us be safe people for others. Read the excerpt from *You're Already Amazing* that begins with "Imagine we're on a playground. . . ."

   Tip: Tell the group that for the next section, everyone will go in a circle and share their answers. Explain that this is so they all can get to know each other better and have fun learning about who God made them. Emphasize there are no "right" or "wrong" responses—they're simply ways to describe how we're all unique. If someone feels like more than one of the categories fits them, that's totally okay. It's also fine if they feel like none of them do. If that's the case, you can ask, "How would you describe yourself?"

   Have each person share what they chose for Setting, Structure, Sight, and Sphere of Needs. Then ask them to share their answer to question 5. Try to affirm what they say and encourage others to do so as well. Wrap up this time by having someone read 1 Corinthians 12:14–18.

6. *Next steps.* Give group members an opportunity to share a response to the "Your Next Step" prompt. Tell them they can also ask a question instead of responding to the prompt. If you have extra time left, spend it getting to know each other better.

7. *Watch Video 4:2.* About ten minutes before the group time is over, the main facilitator will share a few thoughts and play the

closing video. When the video is done, the main facilitator will do whatever else is needed to wrap up the session (such as giving instructions for the following session, sharing prayer requests, offering final encouraging words, transitioning to the Get Creative activity, etc.).

8. *Get creative.* If your group is doing a social activity as suggested in the More LifeGrowth section, then here are two ways to do so. First, before meeting for this session, you can tell your group there will be a social time afterward (example: everyone bringing food or going out for lunch). Or you can plan a time outside your normal group meeting to get together (example: going to a local coffee shop, having a girls' night out, doing a craft, or spending time at someone's home). You know what your group will enjoy most, so be as creative as you'd like and also involve them in the planning if possible.

   If you're a co-facilitator, your main facilitator will communicate with you about the social activity. You may get together as a large group or by tables.

   I'd love to see pictures of your group getting together! You can share them with me on Facebook or Instagram and use the hashtag #alreadyamazing.

Session 5: God's Purpose for Our Lives

1. *Welcome.* (If you're in a large group, the main facilitator will do this segment.) Of all the sessions in this LifeGrowth Guide, this one is the most essential. It brings together everything that has been covered so far and forms the foundation for finishing strong. I've seen how the LIFE statements women write can become a transformative tool. To begin your time together, ask the participants what has stood out to them so far in the LifeGrowth Guide and what God has been teaching them through your time together. Pray and commit this session to him, then watch Video 5:1.

2. *Introduction.* (If you're a co-facilitator, your role will begin here and you will guide your table group through the rest of the material.) Go through "A Brief Review" as a group. Have each person quickly share their answers. If they need clarity about any of these pieces, talk them through their questions so they're ready to create LIFE statements.

3. *LIFE statements.* Move next to the LIFE statement part of the session and have someone read Matthew 22:37–39 as a reminder of why this matters. Then invite each woman to share her LIFE statement with the group. Going in a circle is recommended, but give people permission to pass. When everyone is done, transition to question 1.

    Tip: Remind group members that their LIFE statements are something they'll likely wrestle with and all that's needed right now is a rough draft. If someone is feeling stuck, offer the group's help. Sometimes different perspectives can provide what's missing. Take as much time on LIFE statements as you need to. This is the most important part of the entire LifeGrowth Guide.

4. *Expectations and plans.* Explain that even when we have a LIFE statement, we can get pulled into the expectations of others. Then invite women to share some of their answers to question 2. Transition to the Creating Your "Do What You Can Plan" section. For this part, have women in the group pair up and go through their "Do What You Can Plans" together. When they're done, ask them to choose a way and time to follow up with each other for encouragement and accountability. For example, they could send each other a text during the week.

5. *Approaches to change.* Go in a circle and let each person share her approach to change as well as phrases that especially sound like her from the descriptions. Have fun with this section and keep it lighthearted. Then ask group members to discuss question 3. Explain that we often have similar obstacles, so hearing ideas will help everyone.

6. *Next steps.* Give group members an opportunity to share a response to the "Your Next Step" prompt. Tell them they can also ask a question instead of responding to the prompt. If you have extra time left, spend it getting to know each other better.

7. *Watch Video 5:2.* About ten minutes before the group time is over, the main facilitator will share a few thoughts and play the closing video. When the video is done, the main facilitator will do whatever else is needed to wrap up the session (such as giving instructions for the following session, sharing prayer requests, offering final encouraging words, transitioning to the Get Creative activity, etc.).

8. *Get creative.* If your group is doing the LIFE statement activity suggested in the More LifeGrowth section, there are two ways to do so. First, you can transition to it at this point. Or you can start the craft at the beginning and work on it while you go through the questions and videos. If you're a co-facilitator, your main facilitator will let you know what to do.

Session 6: How We Can Thrive for a Lifetime

1. *Welcome.* (If you're in a large group, the main facilitator will do this segment.) It's the last session! I'm so proud of you for guiding your group to this point. We'll wrap up by talking through how we can thrive as long as God has us on this earth. To help your group start thinking about what a life well lived looks like, ask them, "Who is one of your heroes and why?" Then open in prayer and watch Video 6:1.

2. *Introduction.* (If you're a co-facilitator, your role will begin here and you will guide your table group through the rest of the material.) Start by reading the introduction for the session out loud. Ask group members to underline or highlight phrases that stand out to them as it is read.

3. *Legacy*. Ask question 1 and be ready to answer first. This is a subject that can be hard to talk about, but it's important for group members to have a long-term vision for their lives.

   After finishing question 1, ask someone to read the paragraph that begins, "Ironically. . . ." Then invite women to share some examples of "withdrawals" and "deposits" from the My Heart's Bank Account tool. Follow that up by brainstorming different ways to proactively put deposits in our bank accounts based on the Creating Your Personal Investment Plan tool. Remind them that hearing each other's answers is helpful and encourage them to add new ideas to what they've already written.

4. *LifeGrowth Guide review*. Tell your group you're proud of them for coming so far and working so hard. Then go through the review questions for each session together. When you're done, ask everyone to fill in a date for the next time they'll do a review and add it to their calendars if they haven't already.

   Tip: Take time to invite questions and discussion as you go through the review. It's important for people to tie up any "loose ends" so they can freely move forward when the LifeGrowth Guide is complete. Offer lots of affirmation and encouragement along the way.

5. *Reflection questions*. Answer questions 2 through 4 together. If your group feels comfortable doing so, actually pause and take time to pray out loud together on question 3. You might go in a circle and have each person share one blessing and praise in prayer.

6. *Final thoughts*. Ask someone to read Ephesians 3:17–19. Then ask someone else to read the quote from *You're Already Amazing* that starts with "You're already amazing because. . . ." Invite the group to share final thoughts, questions, or encouragement.

7. *Watch Video 6:2*. About ten minutes before the group time is over, the main facilitator will share a few thoughts and play the closing video. When the video is done, the main facilitator will do

whatever else is needed to wrap up the session (such as sharing prayer requests, offering final encouraging words, transitioning to the Get Creative activity, etc.).

8. *Get creative.* My hope is that every woman who goes through this LifeGrowth Guide will in some way pass on what she's received. As a group, you can spend some time brainstorming about different ways to do so. Answer this question together: "What are some ways we can individually and as a group encourage other women to embrace who they are and become all God created them to be?" You can also have each person in your group complete the collage they've created by adding a "Pay It Forward" piece that shares how they'll pass on what they've received.

   I'd also encourage you to have a celebration time on this day with fun food and decorations (you can keep it really simple and ask for help from your group). Finishing this LifeGrowth Guide is a huge accomplishment and something to be happy about together. If you're a co-facilitator, your main facilitator will communicate with you about any celebration plans.

   I'd love to have a photo of your group from your final meeting day! You can share one with me on Facebook or Instagram and use the hashtag #alreadyamazing.

Connecting with God

You may have read the prayer at the beginning of this book and thought, "I'm not sure I have that kind of relationship with God yet. Can I really talk to God like he's my loving Father and a true friend?" The answer is, "Yes!" God loves you, and he wants you to have a close relationship with him.

God is the one who makes you amazing. "You created my inmost being; you knit me together in my mother's womb. I praise you because I am fearfully and wonderfully made; your works are wonderful, I know that full well" (Ps. 139:13–14).

Yet this is also true: "All have sinned and fall short of the glory of God" (Rom. 3:23). It only takes one sin to separate us from God and for us to fall short of who he created us to be.

Thankfully, God offers a solution for our sin because he loves us so much. Jesus died on the cross so that we could be forgiven and fully become all he made us to be. "If anyone is in Christ, the new creation has come: The old has gone, the new is here!" (2 Cor. 5:17).

To receive what God has done for us, we can simply pray . . .

God,
   Thank you for creating me and pursuing my heart. I know I'm not perfect, so I'm asking you to forgive me and be my Savior. You

gave your life for me, and now I give mine to you. I'm so glad you love me. I love you too. In Jesus's name, amen.

That little prayer not only changes your life—it changes your eternity. You can trust that God heard the desire of your heart and answered it. I encourage you to tell someone about your relationship with God so they can help you move forward in your faith. This LifeGrowth Guide will be an important tool in your spiritual growth too.

As you follow God each day, he will transform you and your life through the power of the Holy Spirit who now lives within you. "Being confident of this, that he who began a good work in you will carry it on to completion until the day of Christ Jesus" (Phil. 1:6).

I'm so thrilled to call you my amazing sister in Jesus!

Acknowledgments

I've thought about groups a lot as I've created this LifeGrowth Guide, and it's made me even more grateful for the tribe of people in my life who have made this project possible.

Thank you to my publishing team: Twila Bennett, Jennifer Leep, Claudia Marsh, Michele Misiak, and Wendy Wetzel. You've had the vision for what the message of *You're Already Amazing* could do in the hearts of women from the very beginning. This LifeGrowth Guide would never have happened without you, and I'm so grateful to call you friends as well as publishing partners. Jen, thank you for the extra time you took to go through this LifeGrowth Guide with me. Our conversations and your insights added so much to this project.

Mark Gerth, you have had to listen to more conversations about the hearts of women than any man should in a lifetime! Thank you for being my rock, biggest fan, strongest supporter, and most faithful encourager. I love sharing life with you, and I'm grateful every day that God brought us together.

My dear friends, you have taught me how to embrace who I truly am and have cheered me on as I continue becoming all God created me to be. Thank you for all the talks over coffee, Skype conversations, Voxer messages, emails, and more. You are gifts from God's heart to mine.

To readers of *You're Already Amazing*: It's still hard to believe there are about a hundred thousand of you out there! One of the parts of heaven I'm looking forward to most is time to connect with each and every one of you. Until then, know that you have a special place in my heart. You laid the foundation for this LifeGrowth Guide, and it wouldn't have happened without you.

Most of all, I'm thankful for you, Jesus. Everything I am and all I have is because of you. You've seen me at my best as well as worst and loved me through both. It's a privilege to catch a glimpse of your affection for all your daughters as I write and a delight to pass that along to them. I pray we will all be strong, faithful, amazing women who bring you joy.

Notes

1. *Baker Evangelical Dictionary of Biblical Theology*, ed. Walter A. Elwell (Grand Rapids: Baker, 1996), s.v. "heart." Available online at http://www.biblestudytools.com/dictionary/heart/.

2. Gary Oliver, "Christian Foundations in Counseling," lecture, John Brown University, Siloam Springs, AR, 2007.

3. Jennifer Warner, "No Joke: Laughter Is Universal," *WebMD Health News*, January 25, 2010, http://www.webmd.com/balance/news/20100125/no-joke-laughter-is-universal?src=RSS_PUBLIC.

4. Holley Gerth, *Opening the Door to Your God-Sized Dream: 40 Days of Encouragement for Your Heart* (Grand Rapids: Revell, 2013), 68–70.

5. See Bill Dedman and Paul Clark Newell Jr., *Empty Mansions: The Mysterious Life of Huguette Clark and the Spending of a Great American Fortune* (New York: Random House, 2013).

Holley Gerth is a *Wall Street Journal* bestselling author, certified life coach, and speaker. She loves Jesus and enjoys encouraging the hearts of women through her popular blog as well as books like *You're Already Amazing*, *You're Going to Be Okay*, and *You're Loved No Matter What*. She's also cofounder of (in)courage.me and a writer for DaySpring, and she has a master's degree in counseling. Holley lives with her husband, Mark, in the South. Connect with Holley at www.holleygerth.com.

More exciting ways to enjoy

Revell
a division of Baker Publishing Group
www.RevellBooks.com

You're Already Amazing!

Grab a friend (or more than one!) and your favorite beverage and gather 'round to learn more about your unique identity as a child of God as well as practical ways to bring change into your relationships and daily lives.

The *You're Already Amazing LifeGrowth Guide* (based on the book *You're Already Amazing*) will lead you through a six-week study with:

- *free videos at HolleyGerth.com/amazing or available on DVD for easy access*

- *questions for groups to discuss or individuals to reflect on*

- *interactive tools based on Holley's training as a counselor and life coach to help you apply what you you're reading*

- *optional creative activities you can do with a group or on your own*

- *prompts for personal journaling*

"I often say it doesn't have to be perfect to be beautiful.
Holley Gerth shows women that's just as true
for our hearts as it is for every other area of our lives."

—Myquillyn Smith, The Nester, author of *The Nesting Place*

Revell
a division of Baker Publishing Group
www.RevellBooks.com

Available wherever books and ebooks are sold.

Discover the dreams God has given you—
and then dare to pursue them.

Holley Gerth takes you by the heart and says, "Yes! You can do this!"
She guides you with insightful questions, action plans to take
the next steps, and most of all, the loving hand of a friend.

Revell
a division of Baker Publishing Group
www.RevellBooks.com

Available wherever books and ebooks are sold.

Connect with Holley at
HolleyGerth.com